Contents

Part 1

Introduction

Yeats's life and work

The poet William Butler Yeats was born on 13 June 1865 at 'George's Ville', No. 1, Sandymount Avenue, Dublin. His father, John Butler Yeats, had been expected to follow the careers of his father and his grandfather and become a Church of Ireland clergyman, but he opted for the law and trained as a barrister before deciding to become an artist. The poet's mother, born Susan Pollexfen, was a member of a well-to-do family in Sligo, in the west of Ireland, which owned ships and a milling company. At the time of his son's birth John Butler Yeats was living on rents from 300 acres of inherited land in County Kildare. As a landlord, about to become a barrister, he had seemed a most acceptable son-in-law to the Polexfens. But when he moved to London in 1867 to study painting and the income from the heavily mortgaged lands diminished, Susan and the children (after W.B. came two daughters and the youngest son, Jack, who later became a famous artist; another son, Robert, died in 1873) spent much time with her parents in Sligo because John Butler Yeats was impractical where money was concerned. He failed to charge enough for his portraits and often went on painting and repainting them for too long. Thus Yeats grew up in an atmosphere of genteel poverty; like so many Irish writers, he had well-to-do, better-off relatives, but in his own family money was always short.

By 1880 the income from the family lands in Kildare finally ceased, and the family moved back to Ireland. From 1875 to 1880 Willie Yeats had been at the Godolphin School in Hammersmith; from 1880 to 1883 he went to the High School, Dublin, learning much about poetry from his father when both of them took the train from Howth – the peninsula forming the northern arm of Dublin Bay – to the city, to breakfast together at the artist's studio near the boy's school. Then came the question of a career – Willie was unlikely to pass the easy entrance examination to Trinity College Dublin, so he entered the School of Art in Dublin: then he decided that he wanted to be a poet and his father encouraged him in this, making light of the need to earn a living. 'A gentleman is not concerned with getting-on' he would say, somewhat fecklessly, making the best of the poverty to which he had condemned his family. Instead of financial security, he gave his children the stimulus of ideas in endlessly challenging conversations, and he encouraged them to develop their own talents.

In Dublin Willie Yeats met John O'Leary (see p. 30) who interested him in nationalism and translations of Irish writing into English: by doing so he gave him fresh and exciting subject matter for his poetry and a new purpose. Not only would he write about the places, the stories, the supernatural beliefs he met in Sligo, but he would give the old Irish legends new expression in English, recreating, he thought, Ireland's largely forgotten intellectual heritage. He was stimulated by reading Sir Samuel Ferguson's translations, as well as James Clarence Mangan's versions of Irish poems, and Standish O'Grady's histories and fiction. His own treatment of material from Irish legend bloomed in *The Wanderings of Oisin* (1889).

1889 was the year he met Maud Gonne, tall and beautiful, a well-to-do revolutionary with whom he fell in love. Penniless, he could only offer poetic devotion: he wrote a play, *The Countess Kathleen*, for her, and many love poems, wistful and melancholic. In 1891 he proposed to her but was refused in the words Maud Gonne used subsequently on many similar occasions; the world would thank her for not marrying him, they should continue to be friends, and he should go on writing lovely poetry for her.

He joined the Theosophists (who believed that knowledge of God could be attained through spiritual ecstasy and direct intuition), only to be asked to leave because of his desire for evidence. Yeats also became interested in what was then considered unorthodox thought: Buddhism, magic, spiritualism, astrology, the Cabbala. He joined the Order of the Golden Dawn, a Rosicrucian order, in 1890. He edited Blake, he read Swedenborg and Boehme. This side of his life he kept apart from his poetry at first; his prose consisted of articles on and reviews of Irish literature, and collections of Irish fairy and folk tales. In 1891 he thought the time ripe, after the death of Parnell had brought a lull to Irish politics, for launching a literary movement, and he formed Irish literary societies in Dublin and London. He told Maud Gonne what he was doing for Ireland was as important as the political work of more obvious nationalists, though for a time he and she became members of the Irish Republican Brotherhood, a secret revolutionary organisation.

During the eighteen-nineties Yeats's poetry became more obscure. He moved from relatively simple poems about Irish places, fairy legends, Indian and pastoral poetry, to poetry using the material of the Irish cycles of tales, the stories of Ulster and the Fenian tales, developing readers' awareness of the heroes and heroines of these legends – Fergus, Conchubar, Cuchulain and Naoise; Maeve, Emer and Deirdre. His book of poems and stories *The Celtic Twilight* (1893) gave its name to the kind of literature produced by Yeats himself and his imitators: romantic, affirmative, sometimes vague, misty, dreamy, and wistful. Yeats was using his 'Celtic' material in a more and more complex visionary way; he had to explain the meanings of his poems in increasingly lengthy notes, glossing his Irish material, explaining, for instance, such names as Tuatha da Danaan, Sidhe or Aengus, discussing the symbolism of the Rose, and relating the contents of poems to the beliefs of country people and those beliefs in turn to other traditions such as vegetation myths or fertility rites. *The Wind Among the Reeds* (1899) is the culmination of this 'Celtic' poetry, mysterious, vague and beautiful.

Yeats's life changed towards the end of the century. He met Lady Gregory in London in 1894, first visited her in Ireland in 1896, and from 1897 tended to spend his summers at Coole Park, her house in County Galway. She lent him money so that he was able to give up the journalism which brought him a minute income (never over about £150 a year before 1900), and concentrate on his own writing. He repaid her loans later out of the proceeds of lecturing in America. He had left the family home in Bedford Park, London, in 1896, sharing rooms for a time with his friend Arthur Symons in the Temple, then renting his own set of rooms in Woburn Buildings in London. The summers at Coole, however, gave him a peaceful ordered existence, and Lady Gregory invited other writers to the house, among them Yeats's friend George Russell (1867-1935) whose pen-name was Æ, George Bernard Shaw (1856-1950), George Moore (1852-1933) and many other Irish authors and artists. She also rekindled his interest in folk tales and speech, and he encouraged her in her excellent translations of the Irish tales, the best known being *Cuchulain of Muirthemne* (1902) and *Gods and Fighting Men* (1904).

Yeats's unrequited love for Maud Gonne had made him increasingly unhappy during the nineties; he had become disillusioned with the Irish nationalists and with the revolutionaries (particularly after seeing the effects of rioting in Dublin in 1897). In 1903 Maud Gonne's marriage to John MacBride put an end to his hopes that one day she would marry him. The love poetry he continued to write still recorded his love for her, but it had become a love which had no future. The 'old high way of love' was replaced by realism, by knowledge of how she had never really understood his aims, of how he had grown out of fashion 'like an old song'. And yet the poems continue to celebrate her beauty, her stature, and the fineness of spirit he had discerned in her. His poetry had begun to develop a new style, stripped of decoration, where nouns and verbs became more telling than adjectives, where the poet might 'wither into truth'.

Yeats found work which was to employ his energies: 'theatre business, management of men'. With Lady Gregory's considerable aid he brought an Irish Theatre into being. They were helped by George Moore and Edward Martyn at first, then by John Millington Synge (1871-1909). Irish plays, first staged in halls, found a permanent home in the Abbey Theatre in Dublin, converted out of a former morgue, and financed in its initial years by an Englishwoman, Annie Horniman. Yeats was Manager of the Abbey from its inception in 1904 until 1910. It was not easy work, and it was not aided by those who objected on religious grounds to Yeats's *The Countess Cathleen* and on puritanical-nationalist grounds to Synge's plays which did not, they thought, portray Ireland as she should be portrayed. This led, in the case of Synge's *The Playboy of the Western World*, to riots in 1907 which disillusioned Yeats deeply, though he insisted on staging Synge's play; it seemed to him that many of the public disliked the art he and his friends were working so hard to write and produce.

After this Lady Gregory, her son Robert, and Yeats went to Italy; it was his first visit and a revelation of what enlightened aristocratic patronage had done for the arts in Italy. Here was a vital contrast: between the mob howling down great art in Ireland, and what had been created by aristocratic patrons in Urbino and Florence, in Sienna and Ravenna. But Yeats was to experience still more disillusion with Ireland, for when Lady Gregory's nephew, Sir Hugh Lane (1875-1915), offered his superb collection of French paintings to Dublin, the Corporation cavilled at the gift which Lane had made conditional upon his pictures being properly housed. (He himself favoured a design for a gallery over the River Liffey.) Yeats hurled himself into the controversy that arose, and began to write angry political poems contrasting Irish patrons with past Italian ducal munificence and vision. He contrasted, too, Irish nationalists with those of the past, to the denigration of contemporary leaders.

'All changed, changed utterly', wrote Yeats in 'Easter 1916', deeply moved by the unexpected rising in Ireland which, as he realised, made martyrs of the leaders executed for their part in it. He had been in France when it occurred, staying with Maud Gonne in her house in Normandy. Her marriage had lasted but two years; she obtained a separation from MacBride, and retired from public life. She had a child, Sean, by MacBride, and had had two children earlier by Lucien Millevoye (a French journalist and follower of General Boulanger), a boy who died in 1891 and a girl, Iseult, born in 1894. MacBride was one of the leaders executed in Dublin, and Yeats proposed marriage to Maud again, to be refused in her customary way. Later he proposed to Iseult who enjoyed flirting with him and would not give him an answer. He returned to France in 1917 to propose again. This time he issued an ultimatum to Iseult; when she came to London she must say yea or nay – if the latter he would marry a girl whom he had known for some years. Iseult refused him, and he married Georgie Hyde-Lees on 20 October 1917. She was twenty-six, he fifty-two, and the marriage transformed his life.

Shortly after their marriage Mrs Yeats took up automatic writing, and Yeats was greatly excited by this, as it seemed to offer him a system of thought. He wrote to his father that 'the setting of it all in order' had helped him with his verse, 'has given me a new framework and new patterns'. *A Vision* (1925) incorporated in its system his ideas on history and human personality. His *Collected Works* had appeared in an eight-volume edition in 1908, and it might have seemed his poetic career was over, but now that he was working on *A Vision* his poetry took on new life. The disillusionment which had marked the poems of *The Green Helmet* (1910) and *Responsibilities* (1914) and some of the poems of *The Wild Swans at Coole* (1919) gave way to a new creativity, in which Yeats incorporated the beauty of his early poetry along with the bare strength he had learned to express in his middle period, achieving the rich texture of his mature manner.

He found new confidence in his marriage which had assured the continuance of the Yeats line, for two children, Anne and Michael, were born in 1919 and 1921 respectively. His marriage was romantically based on the first house Yeats owned, his tower in the west of Ireland, and practically on the subsequent purchase of a fine house in Merrion Square, Dublin; and his new confidence was grounded in what Yeats praised in 'Under Saturn' as the wisdom his wife had brought to their marriage, the comfort she had made. There was, in addition, the international public recognition given to his poetry by the award of the Nobel Prize, in 1923, and that given to his standing as an Irish public man by his appointment as a Senator of the newly created Irish Free State. The poetry of *Michael Robartes and the Dancer* (1921) included not only 'Easter 1916' but 'The Second Coming' with its bleak anticipation of coming ruin and chaos, and 'A Prayer for my Daughter', with its hope that his daughter might avoid the errors of such opinionated beauties as Maud Gonne and follow instead the courtesy and glad kindness he appreciated in his young wife.

The Tower (1928) contained a magnificent range of poems: personal in such things as the particular meanings he attached to the city of Byzantium in 'Sailing to Byzantium', the local history and legend attaching to his tower in County Galway and its neighbourhood, but universal in their treatment of the human problems of age; the descent of inherited characteristics in families; the bitterness of civil war; and the whole question, in 'Among School Children', of the meaning of life itself. There were poems which continued the matter of *A Vision*, such as 'Two Songs from a Play' or 'Leda and the Swan' as well as poems of past love, and poems in the series *A Man Young and Old* expressing love as if a man young and old were speaking them, balanced by the later series *A Woman Young and Old* in *The Winding Stair and other Poems* (1933).

This volume reflects Yeats's interest in the Irish writers of the eighteenth century, whom he had come to read after his marriage. His Irish reading in his twenties and thirties had been of translations of Irish literature or of authors known more in Ireland than outside it – Irish novelists, for instance, such as Carleton, the Banims, Kickham, and Emily Lawless. In his middle period he had been rereading Shakespeare and rereading and editing Spenser, as well as studying Chaucer and discovering Landor and Donne. But he found his true intellectual ancestry in Swift (whom he had earlier not regarded as Irish), Berkeley, Goldsmith and Burke. He paid tribute to them not only in poems such as 'The Seven Sages', but in his prose, notably in the Introduction to *The Words upon the Window-Pane* – included in *Wheels and Butterflies* (1934) – his superbly realistic, atmospheric play about a seance and the ghostly presence of Swift. His *Four Plays for Dancers* (1921) had been designed, under the influence of Japanese Noh drama, for small select audiences, but later some of his plays were again written for and produced in the Abbey.

In the nineteen-twenties and thirties Yeats's health caused anxiety: high blood pressure in 1924, a bleeding lung in 1927, Malta fever in 1929, the Steinach operation in 1934, heart missing a beat and nephritis in 1936. None of this diminished his output, though it meant the abandonment of the tower (damp and not very comfortable) as a summer residence after 1929, and subsequent winter visits south in search of sunshine to France, Italy and Spain. Lady Gregory died in 1932 and the Yeats family then gave up the Dublin town house in Merrion Square, leasing for thirteen years a small old farmhouse with attractive grounds at Rathfarnham at the foot of the Dublin mountains. Yeats had made new friends in England and visited Lady Gerald Wellesley in Cornwall in 1937 and 1938 and the Heald sisters in Sussex in 1938. His last public appearance was in the Abbey Theatre in August 1938; he died at Roquebrune in France on 28 January 1939, still writing poetry within days of his death.

A note on the text

Yeats revised his poems frequently. The changes he made can be most easily found in the 884-page volume entitled *The Variorum Edition of the Poems of W.B. Yeats,* ed. Peter Allt and Russell K. Alspach,

Macmillan Company, New York, 1957. W.B. Yeats, *The Poems: A New Edition* (1984) even incorporates some changes made (for an abortive American edition of his poems to be published by Scribner's) by Yeats shortly before his death. Several scholars have written on some of the alterations he made in the process of composition: their books include Curtis Bradford, *Yeats at Work*, Southern Illinois University Press, Illinois, 1965; David R. Clark, *Yeats At Songs and Choruses*, Colin Smythe, Gerrard's Cross, 1983; Jon Stallworthy, *Between the Lines: Yeats's Poetry in the Making*, Clarendon Press, Oxford, 1963, and *Vision and Revision in Yeats's Last Poems*, Clarendon Press, Oxford, 1963.

These Notes are linked to W.B. Yeats, *Selected Poetry*, Pan Books, London, 1974 and subsequent printings, which is readily available and inexpensive. It follows the text and arrangement of the *Collected Poems*, Macmillan, London, 2nd edn, 1950. Yeats agreed to divide his poems for the *Collected Poems* of 1933 into *Lyrical* and *Narrative and Dramatic* categories, and these divisions have been continued in *Collected Poems* (1950), 2nd edn, and *The Poems: A New Edition*, Macmillan, London, 1984.

'Adam's Curse', not included in *Selected Poetry*, is discussed here. *Selected Poetry*, because of lack of space, does not include any of the longer poems from the category of *Narrative and Dramatic*, but a representative, fully annotated selection of these narrative and dramatic poems is included in *Poems of W.B. Yeats: A New Selection*, Macmillan, London, 1984. Some minor poems included in *Selected Poetry* are not discussed in these Notes since space does not permit this; they are, however, explained in the present author's *A New Commentary on the Poems of W.B. Yeats*, Macmillan, London, 1984.

Part 2

Summaries
of SELECTED POEMS

Poems from *Crossways* (1889)

This heading was first used for a group of poems in *Poems* (1895), most of them taken from *The Wanderings of Oisin* (1889). The poems were written when Yeats was trying 'many pathways'.

'The Stolen Child'

In this poem, first published in 1886, Yeats is moving away from the Indian and Arcadian poems with which he began writing (you will find them in *Collected Poems* and *The Poems. A New Edition*: they include 'The Song of the Happy Shepherd', 'The Sad Shepherd', 'Anashuya and Vijaya', 'The Indian upon God' and 'The Indian to his Love') to Irish material. This poem is set in Sligo, the names of places locating it firmly there. And it reflects Yeats's interest in the belief in the supernatural that he found among the people in the west of Ireland, in particular the idea that the fairies carried off children from the human world. The poem is not so much escape from the 'real' world as escape into fairyland. Yeats called it not 'the poetry of insight and knowledge' that he hoped to write but poetry of 'longing and complaint'.

NOTES AND GLOSSARY:

Sleuth Wood in the lake: Sleuth Wood (*Irish* sliu, a slope). Yeats alludes to it elsewhere by its more usual name Slish Wood (*Irish* slios, inclined); it runs along the lower slopes of the Killery mountains at the edge of Lough Gill, County Sligo

Rosses: Rosses, Rosses Point, a seaside village about five miles from Sligo, where the Yeats family spent summer holidays with Pollexfen and Middleton cousins. Yeats described Further Rosses as 'a very noted fairy locality' in a note on the poem, and in *Mythologies*, pp. 88-9, described a corner of it as being a place where the Sidhe or fairies might carry off a man's sould if he fell asleep there

Glen-Car: Glen-Car and Glen-Car Lough (Glen of the Standing Stone), with several waterfalls, between Ben Bulben and Cope's Mountain, County Sligo

'Down by the Salley Gardens'

Yeats described the poem, first published in *The Wanderings of Oisin* (1889) and originally entitled 'An Old Song Re-Sung', as an attempt to reconstruct an old song from three lines imperfectly remembered by an old peasant woman in the village of Ballisodare, County Sligo, who often sings them to herself. These two stanzas are probably the source:

Down by the Sally Gardens my own true love and I did meet;
She passed the Sally Gardens, a tripping with her snow white feet.
She bid me take life easy just as leaves fall from each tree
But I being young and foolish with my true love would not agree.

In a field by the river my lovely girl and I did stand
And leaning on her shoulder I pressed her burning hand,
She bid me take life easy, just as the stream flows o'er the weirs
But I being young and foolish I parted her that day in tears.

NOTES AND GLOSSARY:

salley: willow. There are salley gardens on the Ballisodare river, County Sligo, near the mills formerly owned by the Pollexfen family; the willow was used for scollops in the thatched roofs of the houses there

Poems from *The Rose* (1893)

The Rose was a heading first used by Yeats in *Poems* (1895) for a group of shorter poems, included earlier in his *The Countess Kathleen and Various Legends and Lyrics* (1892). *The Rose* had various symbolic meanings; as a title it probably means the 'Eternal Rose of Beauty and of Peace'. It also was used in the sense of a rose in love poetry, and Yeats knew Irish poets had used it to symbolise Ireland (as in the 'little black rose' of Aubrey De Vere (1814-1902), or the 'Dark Rosaleen' of James Clarence Mangan). It was also used to symbolise the Rose of Friday in Irish poetry. Yeats's membership of the Order of the Golden Dawn gave him other symbolic meanings. In the Rosicrucian symbolism the four leaves of the Rose and the Cross make a mystic marriage, the rose feminine, the cross masculine; the rose blooms on the sacrifice of the cross. So the Rose symbolised spiritual beauty,

and love, and Ireland, and intellectual beauty – and Maud Gonne, with whom he had fallen in love in 1889.

'Fergus and the Druid'

This poem, first published in May 1892, and extensively revised, deals with Fergus MacRoy (or MacRoigh), a legendary king of Ulster, who married Ness (or Nessa). She persuaded him to allow her son by a previous marriage, Conor MacNessa, to rule for a year in his stead, and effectively tricked him out of his kingdom at the end of the year. Yeats found his material in Sir Samuel Ferguson's (1810-86) poem 'The Abdication of Fergus MacRoy'. Fergus lived out his days hunting, fighting and feasting. He was a poet and in the Irish saga, the *Tain bo Cuailgne*, he was the lover of Maeve, Queen of Connaught.

NOTES AND GLOSSARY:

shape to shape: shape-changing is a feature of Irish mythology

***Druid*:** Druids were priests, prophets, wise men and magicians

Red Branch kings: the Red Branch heroes who served Conchubar (or Conor. Yeats also used the spellings Conhor, Concobar and Concubar), the king of Ulster; they lived at Emain Macha (*Irish*, the Twins of Macha, who was an Irish horse goddess), his capital near modern Armagh

subtle Conchubar: the adjective conveys something of the king's character, which emerged in the tale of 'The Fate of the Children of Usna'. He wanted to marry Deirdre, a young girl who was the daughter of Felimid, his harper. She was hidden away in the hills in the charge of an old nurse, Lavarcham, but fell in love with Naoise, one of the Red Branch heroes. They ran away, and went to Scotland with Naoise's brothers Ainnle and Ardan, the other children of Usna. Fergus (see above) was sent as a guarantor of safe conduct to bring them back, Conchubar having promised there would be no reprisals. Fergus, however, was under *geasa* (an Irish word with a meaning something akin to *tabu*) never to refuse an invitation to a feast, and Conchubar arranged that Barach, another Red Branch hero, should invite him to one, and in his absence the children of Usna were killed treacherously by Conchubar

quern: apparatus for grinding corn, usually made of two circular stones, the upper one turned by hand

slate-coloured thing: the bag of dreams

'Cuchulain's Fight with the Sea'

This poem, first published in 1892, and extensively revised, deals with the death of Cuchulain (Yeats also spelled the name as Cuhoollin and Cuchullin; he pronounced it Cuhoolin. It should, however, be pronounced Cu-hullin). His name (Cu Culann) means the Hound of Culann; he was sometimes called the Hound of Ulster. The name was given to him by Cathbad the Druid because, having made his way to Conchubar's court at the age of seven, he killed the fierce hound of Culann (or Culain) the smith in self-defence, and said that in compensation he would undertake its work of protecting the smith's flocks and other possessions. He was originally called Setanta, and was the son of Sualtin and Dechtire (Conchubar's sister). In the tales he is the greatest of the heroes of the Red Branch, famous for his fighting ability and prodigious strength.

NOTES AND GLOSSARY:

Emer: Cuchulain's wife, Emer of Borda, the daughter of Forgael. His wooing of her is told in *The Book of the Dun Cow*. Yeats derived this poem from oral tradition, a ninth-century tale in *The Yellow Book of Lecan* and Jeremiah Curtin's *Myths and Folklore of Ireland* (1890). In *The Yellow Book of Lecan* version Cuchulain's son is called Conlaech, and his mother is Aoife, with whom Cuchulain had an affair when he was in Scotland being trained in fighting with Scathach, an Amazon. Yeats may have confused Emer and Aoife

dun: a fort

raddling . . . raddled: reddening with dye . . . reddened

the web: woven stuff

cars of battle: chariots

one sweet-throated: Eithne Inguba, Cuchulain's young mistress

herd: herdsman, in charge of cattle

Red Branch: see notes on 'Fergus and the Druid'

young sweetheart: Eithne Inguba

Conchubar: see notes on 'Fergus and the Druid'

sweet-throated maid: Eithne Inguba

Druids: see notes on 'Fergus and the Druid'

the horses of the sea: the waves

'The Lake Isle of Innisfree'

This poem, first published in 1890, was written in Bedford Park, the London suburb where the Yeats family lived from 1888 to 1902. Yeats was homesick for Ireland, and hearing in Fleet Street a tinkle of water and seeing a fountain in a shop-window, which balanced a little ball upon its jet, he began to remember the sound of lake water in Ireland.

From this came 'The Lake Isle of Innisfree', which was, he said, his first lyric with anything of his own in its rhythm. His father had read passages from the American author Henry David Thoreau's (1817-62) *Walden* (1854) to him and he thought that he might live alone, as Thoreau had done, in pursuit of wisdom. He thought of living on Innisfree, a rocky island in Lough Gill, County Sligo.

NOTES AND GLOSSARY:

I will arise and go: the phase echoes the Bible, Luke 15:18, 'I will arise and go to my father'

Innisfree: (*Irish*) Heather Island

night and day: the phrase echoes the Bible, Mark 5:5, 'And always, night and day, he was in the mountains'

heart's core: possibly an echo of Shelley, *Adonais*, 1:192, 'thy heart's core'

'The Sorrow of Love'

This poem, first published in 1892, is one of the best-known examples of Yeats's rewriting of his early work. Here, for comparison, is the first stanza of the early version:

> The quarrel of the sparrows in the eaves,
> The full round moon and the star-laden sky,
> And the loud song of the ever-singing leaves
> Had hid away earth's old and weary cry

NOTES AND GLOSSARY:

a girl: presumably Helen of Troy, though the poem also relates to Maud Gonne

Odysseus: Homer's *Odyssey* tells how Odysseus, son of Laertes, King of the island of Ithaca, having taken part in the Greeks' expedition to Troy (which they besieged for ten years before taking it through the stratagem of the wooden horse) spent ten years returning home

Priam: King of Troy, killed after the fall of Troy by Neoptolemus, son of the Greek warrior Achilles. Priam's children included Paris (who caused the Graeco–Trojan war by bringing back to Troy with him Helen, the wife of Menelaus, King of Sparta); Hector (killed by Achilles); and Cassandra (captured after the fall of Troy and brought to Argos as a slave or concubine by Agamemnon, brother of Menelaus, who led the Greek expedition to Troy)

'The White Birds'

This poem was first published in 1892. It was written in 1891, three days after Yeats and Maud Gonne had been walking on the cliffs at Howth, a peninsula forming the northern arm of Dublin Bay, on the day after Yeats had first proposed marriage to her and been rejected. She had told him if she had to be a bird she would be a seagull.

NOTES AND GLOSSARY:

blue star of twilight: Venus

lily and rose: the lily is a masculine symbol, the rose feminine

Danaan: fairy, from the Tuatha de Danaan. (The first printing of the poem was accompanied by a note: 'The birds of fairyland are said to be white as snow. The Danaan islands are the islands of the faeries.' And a later note described the Danaan shore as 'Tier-nan-Oge, or fairy-land'. Tir-na-nOg in Irish means the Land of the Young

'The Man who Dreamed of Faeryland'

This poem, first published in 1891, begins each stanza with a place near Sligo; there is, obviously, a strong autobiographical element in it.

NOTES AND GLOSSARY:

Dromahair: also spelt Drumahair, a village in County Leitrim near Lough Gill; its Irish name Dromdha Eithiar means the ridge of the two demons

world-forgotten isle: probably a fairy paradise, akin to the first island to which the immortal Niamh brought Oisin in Yeats's *The Wanderings of Oisin* (1889)

Lissadell: Lissadell, a barony in County Sligo; the Irish means the fort or courtyard of the blind man. The Gore-Booth family have had their home there since the eighteenth century, the present house having been built in 1832. See 'In Memory of Eva Gore-Booth and Con Markiewicz'

the hill: of Lugnagall (see the fourth stanza), in Irish the Hollow of the Strangers (Yeats thought it meant the Steep Place of the Strangers). Lugnagall is a townland in the Glencar Valley in County Sligo

golden or the silver: solar and lunar principles when fused symbolise perfection; solar is represented by gold, lunar by silver. Notice the 'silver heads' and 'gold morning' of the first stanza, the 'stormy silver' and 'the gold of day' of the third. Yeats is beginning to develop his repeated symbols here, and this repetition enriches the picture of blessedness, of perfection

Scanavin: a townland a mile from Colloney in County Sligo; a well there is called in Irish the well of fine shingle

spired: the word implies spiral movement

Poems from *The Wind among the Reeds* (1899)

This heading was the title of a collection of poems published in 1899, which had extensive notes by Yeats on his source material in Irish legends. The poems are symbolist, melancholic, and full of haunting beauty, of longing and complaint, and of frustrated love.

'The Host of the Air'

This poem, first published in 1893, was originally called 'The Stolen Bride'. Yeats's note gives the source of the poem as 'a Gaelic poem on the subject' which an old woman at Balisodare, County Sligo repeated to him and translated. He always regretted not having taken down the words. He explained in a note that anyone who tastes fairy food or drink is 'glamoured and stolen by the faeries' and that is why Bridget sets O'Driscoll to play cards. She had been swept away by the faeries, the 'folk of the air', in an early version of the poem.

NOTES AND GLOSSARY:

Hart Lake: a small lake in the Ox Mountains in County Sligo

Bridget his bride: in another note (*Later Poems*, 1924) Yeats commented that in the Irish ballad the husband came home to find the Keeners (those mourners who utter the keen (from the Irish *caoinim*, I wail) for the dead at wakes or funerals) lamenting, and thus knew his wife was dead

red wine . . . white bread . . . host of the air: the 'host' in the Eucharist, the Communion Service, is the bread (*hostia* in Latin), the body of Christ. Here Yeats is blending pagan and Christian symbolism

'The Song of Wandering Aengus'

This poem, first published in 1897, deals with the shape-changing of the fairies, the Tuatha de Danaan. It was, however, suggested to Yeats by a Greek folk song, probably 'The Three Fishes' in Lucy Garnett, *Greek Folk Poesy* (1896), but when he wrote it, he was, he said, thinking 'of Ireland and of the spirits that are in Ireland'.

NOTES AND GLOSSARY:

I: Yeats's note on 'He mourns for the change that has come upon him and His Beloved, and longs for the End of the World' explained that the 'man with a hazel wand' in that poem 'may well have been Angus [he spelled the name both Angus and Aengus], Master of Love'. Elsewhere Yeats called him the god of youth, beauty and poetry who ruled in Tir-na-nOg, the country of the young

hazel wand: the hazel was the Irish tree of life or knowledge and Yeats said that in Ireland 'it was doubtless, as elsewhere, the tree of the heavens'

glimmering girl . . . apple blossom: the image suggests Maud Gonne, with whom Yeats associated blossom and particularly apple-blossom. In his *Autobiographies* he described their first meeting when her complexion 'was luminous, like that of apple-blossom through which the light falls and I remember her standing that first day by a great heap of such blossoms in the window' (p.123)

silver apples . . . golden apples: compare the imagery of these lines with their lunar and solar imagery with that in 'The Man who Dreamed of Faeryland'

'He mourns for the change that has come upon him and His Beloved, and longs for the End of the World'

This poem, first published in 1897, had the following note printed after it:

In the old Irish story of Usheen's journey to the Islands of the Young, Usheen sees amid the waters a hound with one red ear, following a deer with no horns; and other persons in other old Celtic stories see the like images of the desire of the man, and of the desire of the woman 'which is for the desire of the man', and of all desires that are as these. The man with the wand of hazel may well have been Angus, Master of Love; and the boar without bristles is the ancient Celtic image of the darkness which will at last destroy the world, as it destroys the sun at nightfall in the west.

NOTES AND GLOSSARY:

white deer . . . hound: Yeats used this image in *The Wanderings of Oisin* and probably got it from a translation by Brian O'Looney of Michael Comyn's Irish poem 'The Lay of Oisin in the Land of Youth'

the Boar: compare this image with that in 'The Valley of the

Black Pig'. These 'apocalyptic' poems about future catastrophic wars foreshadow later poems such as 'The Second Coming', 'Meditations in Time of Civil War' or 'The Gyres', and Yeats, apart from being influenced by the ideas of MacGregor Mathers (see notes upon 'All Souls' Night'), also met the idea among Irish country people, as he records in the second edition of *The Celtic Twilight* (1902)

'The Cap and Bells'

This poem was first published in 1894, and in Yeats's note on it in *The Wind Among the Reeds* he tells us that he dreamed the story exactly as he had written it; it gave him 'the sense of illumination and exaltation that one gets from visions'. The lady is not affected by the jester's offer of his soul (line 3) or his heart (line 13) but by his cap and bells.

'The Valley of the Black Pig'

This poem, when first published in 1896, was annotated by Yeats as follows:

The Irish peasantry have for generations comforted themselves in their misfortunes, with visions of a great battle, to be fought in a mysterious valley called, 'The Valley of the Black Pig', and to break at last the power of their enemies. A few years ago, in the barony of Lisadell, in County Sligo, an old man would fall entranced upon the ground from time to time, and rave out a description of the battle; and I have myself heard [it] said that the girths shall rot from the bellies of the horses, because of the few men that shall come alive out of the valley

A longer note in *The Wind Among the Reeds* called the battle a mythological one, describing the black pig as 'one with the bristleless boar, that killed Dearmod [Diarmuid], in November, upon the western end of Ben Bulben', as well as with other Celtic boars and sows and those in Greek legend. The pig was explained as a symbol of cold and winter battling with the summer, or death battling with life. The battle was to be compared with the battles fought by the Sidhe (the fairies of the wind in Irish mythology), when they are taking away someone, when they fight for the harvest in November, and when the Tuatha de Danaan (the tribes of the goddess Dana, the powers of light, warmth, fruitfulness and goodness) fight the Fomor (the powers of darkness, cold and barrenness, and badness): and these battles were explained as the battle of all things with decay.

NOTES AND GLOSSARY:

cromlech: a prehistoric construction of stones, usually one large stone resting horizontally on several upright ones. There are many in Ireland

grey cairn: this may refer to the cairn on Knocknarea (in Irish 'the hill of the kings' or 'the hill of execution'), a mountain in County Sligo, reputedly the grave of Maeve, queen of Connaught, but more likely that of Eoghan Bel, the last pagan king of Connaught, buried upright there with his spear in his hand

'The Secret Rose'

This poem, first published in 1896, blends pagan and Christian symbolism.

NOTES AND GLOSSARY:

Rose . . . great leaves: the Rosicrucian emblem of the four-leaved rose is probably intended here. Yeats had a vague belief in the possibility of some revelation occurring; it was bound up with his idea of creating an Order of Celtic Mysteries (in which he might establish complete understanding with Maud Gonne). The Rose also suggests the Red Rose or Intellectual Beauty, and Ireland, and Maud Gonne

Holy Sepulchre: the tomb of Jesus Christ in Jerusalem

the . . . Magi: the three wise men who came from the east to attend the birth of Jesus, bringing with them gifts of gold and frankincense and myrrh

the kind who saw . . . in Druid vapour: Yeats's note tells us that he unintentionally changed the story of the death of Conchubar, king of Ulster, who did not see the crucifix in a vision but was told of it. He had been wounded by a ball made of the dried brain of an enemy which lodged in his head and was left there; his head was mended with thread of gold, and he survived for seven years. Then, noticing 'the unusual changes of the creation and the eclipse of the sun and the moon at its full' and asking Bucrach the Druid the reason for this, he was told that Jesus was being crucified, whereon he drew his sword, saying he would kill those who were putting Jesus to death, and began to cut and fell a grove of trees. The excessiveness of his fury caused the ball to burst out of his head and he died

pierced hands . . . rood: those of Christ, nailed to the rood, the Cross

him/Who . . . Fand . . . Emer: in Irish legend, two birds linked with a chain of gold sang the army of Ulster into a magic sleep: the birds turned into two beautiful women and cast a magical weakness on the hero Cuchulain in which he lay for a year. Then Aengus ('probably Aengus the master of love') came and told him that Fand, wife of Mannannan MacLir, master of the sea, loved him, and that she and her sister Laban would heal his magical weakness if he would come to the country of the gods. He did so, and, after being Fand's lover for a month, promised to meet her at a place called 'the Yew at the Strand's End'. He returned to earth, but his wife Emer won his love back, and Mannannan carried Fand off from 'the Yew at Strand's End'. Cuchulain went mad with grief when he saw her going, and wandered in the mountains without food or drink till a druid's drink of forgetfulness cured him

him who drove the gods . . . liss: after the battle of Gabhra (near Garristown in north County Dublin) Caoilte, friend of Oisin, one of the Fianna or Fenians, when all the Fianna were killed, drove the gods out of their liss (a mound or fort) either at Osraighe (Ossory) or at Eas Ruaidh (Assaroe)

barrows: burial places

proud dreaming king: Fergus MacRoigh: see notes on 'Fergus and the Druid' above

him who sold tillage: a young man in 'The Red Pony', a folk tale in William Larminie, *West Irish Folk Tales and Romances* (1893). He finds on the road a box with a light coming from it and a lock of hair inside it. He becomes the servant of a king, and leaves the box in a hole in the wall of the stable where the light from it is strong; he is asked to show the king the box, and is told to find the woman to whom the hair belongs. Finally the young man, not the king, marries her

shining loveliness: the poem was written to Maud Gonne

great wind: probably a reference to the end of the world

'The Fiddler of Dooney'

This poem, first published in 1892, probably was suggested by a blind fiddler, James Howley, who played the music for outdoor country dances, held at Dooney Rock (the Irish name is Dun Aodh, Hugh's Fort) on the shore of Lough Gill, County Sligo.

NOTES AND GLOSSARY:

Kilvarnet: a townland near Ballinacarrow, County Sligo

Mocharabuiee: Mrs Yeats added a footnote to the 1950 *Collected Poems*: 'pronounced as if spelt "Mockrabwee"'. The Irish name means the Yellow Plain, the townland of Magheraboy, south-west of Sligo

Peter: St Peter keeps the keys of the Gate of Heaven

Poems from *In the Seven Woods* (1904)

This is the title of the first book published by Yeats's sister Elizabeth Corbet Yeats at her Dun Emer press. This edition included the long poems 'The Old Age of Queen Maeve' and 'Baile and Aillinn' which show Yeats moving to a new, more direct style. There is a tired air about some of the poems in this volume, published in the year that Maud Gonne married John MacBride in 1903, noticeable in poems such as 'Never Give All the Heart', 'O Do not love too long' and 'Under the Moon'. The poem which conveys this most clearly is 'Adam's Curse'—which is not included in *Selected Poems* but on which comment is offered below.

'Red Hanrahan's Song about Ireland'

This poem, first published in 1894, does not share in the general mood of the poems of *In the Seven Woods* (which were written later). It was included in a story entitled 'Kathleen-ny-Houlihan' and it may owe something to James Clarence Mangan's poem 'Kathleen-ny-Houlihan', which personified Ireland as Kathleen. It is written to Maud Gonne, who later acted the title-role of Cathleen, the old woman who symbolises a freed Ireland, in Yeats's play *Cathleen-ni-Houlihan* (1902). The poem was strengthened in various revisions.

NOTES AND GLOSSARY:

Red Hanrahan: Hanrahan was a character invented by Yeats, a wandering Irish poet and schoolmaster, probably founded on Eoghan Ruadh O'Sullivan (1748-84) who had a varied career as a poet, schoolmaster, a wandering labourer, a tutor, a sailor in the navy, a soldier, and finally a schoolmaster again. His poems circulated in manuscript and oral tradition and were not published till 1901

Cummen Strand: the southern shore of the Garavogue estuary, north-west of Sligo

left hand: unlucky in Irish and many other traditions
Knocknarea . . . the stones . . . Maeve: see note on 'grey cairn', in 'The Valley of the Black Pig'
Clooth-na-Bare: Lough Ia (in Irish the Lough of the Two Geese) on Sliabh Daene, in Irish Bird Mountain, in County Sligo. Yeats described Cathleen as seeking all over the world a lake deep enough to drown her faery (Yeats usually spelt fairy as faery) life of which she had become weary until she reached the deepest water in the world in Lough Ia. He added in a footnote that Clooth-na-Bare should be Cailleac Beare, meaning the Old Woman Beare (or Bere, or Verah or Dera or Dhera). She was associated with many places in Ireland, notably the megalithic monument of Sliabh Daene, not far from Lough Ia
Holy Rood: the cross

'Adam's Curse'

This poem, first published in 1902, was written to Maud Gonne and the occasion of its writing is discussed in her autobiography *A Servant of the Queen* (see notes below). It marks the emergence of more direct utterance, a nearer approximation to speech, in Yeats's work; while still carrying echoes of his romantic love poetry of the eighteen-nineties, it has a new note of tiredness, almost of disillusion about its insistence upon the need for hard work to create beautiful art and love.

NOTES AND GLOSSARY:
Adam's Curse: after Adam and Eve were expelled from the Garden of Eden (see the Bible, Genesis 3) they had to live by their labour
We . . . mild woman . . . and you and I: Yeats had called on Maud Gonne ('you'), who was staying at the house of her cousins May and Chotie Gonne in South Kensington, London, where her sister Mrs Kathleen Pilcher (that 'mild woman') was also staying. It was after dinner, the sisters were sitting beside each other on a sofa, and Yeats (who considered Maud Gonne overworked and thought that she neglected herself) cast a critical eye on Maud, still in her dark clothes with the black veil she wore instead of a hat when travelling. As she put it, 'he told Kathleen he liked her dress and that she was looking younger than ever. It was on that occasion Kathleen remarked that it was hard work

being beautiful which Willie turned into his poem "Adam's Curse".'

a moment's thought: this quality of nonchalance, of an apparent casualness in the achievement of art, corresponds to *sprezzatura**, the quality Yeats admired in Renaissance figures in Italy. Elsewhere he stressed the difficulty of putting his thoughts and discoveries into rhyme (echoing a remark of William Morris (1834-96), that Yeats quoted on another occasion, about the hard work involved in writing poetry)

stitching and unstitching: Yeats constantly wrote and rewrote his poetry, plays, and prose, and when they were in print he continued to revise much of them in subsequent editions

labour to be beautiful: elsewhere Yeats regarded the achievement of beauty ('the discipline of the looking glass') as one of the most difficult of the arts

compounded of high courtesy: love was a discipline, and had to be created and earned with reference to past achievements, to be approached wisely in 'the old high way of love'

Poems from *The Green Helmet and Other Poems* (1910)

The poems in *The Green Helmet* are varied and transitional; they reveal the poet's greater readiness to write about public matters; and they record how his romantic poetry (and the hopes it conveyed) inspired by and written to Maud Gonne had foundered on her marriage to John MacBride in 1903. There is a static quality about the poetry of this volume, but one that is regretful and poignant. The poetry is being stripped of decoration, and Yeats has not yet found a new voice to reflect his changing life as he becomes immersed in the affairs of the Abbey Theatre.

'No Second Troy'

This poem written in 1908 was first published in 1910 and is one of the most effective poems linking Maud Gonne with Helen of Troy.

NOTES AND GLOSSARY:
her:　　　　　Maud Gonne

*sprezzatura: (*Italian*) a careless rapture, a spontaneous improvisation.

with misery:	by refusing to marry him. He had proposed to her at intervals after 1891 and she always told him the world would thank her for not marrying him, that they should remain close friends. They had a close friendship and for a time a Platonic 'mystic marriage'
of late:	Maud Gonne withdrew from Irish public life for several years after she had sought a divorce and gained a legal separation from her husband in 1906
violent ways:	she had been involved with political activists in the IRB, the Irish Republican Brotherhood (from which she – and Yeats – withdrew about the turn of the century), and was an inflammatory orator
little streets upon the great:	probably a reference to the semi-political clubs out of which the Sinn Fein (the Irish means 'ourselves alone') movement grew. Yeats regarded many Irish nationalist politicians at the time as ignorant and envious, and censorious of art they neither understood nor sympathised with
tightened bow:	an image with sexual meaning in Blake's poetry, and used in Yeats's poem 'The Arrow' in the volume *In the Seven Woods* (1904)
Troy:	Troy was sacked by the Greeks after a ten-year siege: the cause of the war was the carrying off of Helen, wife of Menelaus, King of Sparta, by Paris, one of the sons of Priam, King of Troy

('arrows of desire' -Blake)

'Upon a House shaken by the Land Agitation'

This poem deals with the effects of the settlement of the Irish land question in the late nineteenth century and early twentieth, by a series of acts which culminated in the Wyndham Land Act of 1903. Through this legislation, which had been forced on the British government by agrarian unrest and the work of Michael Davitt's (1846-1906) Irish Land League as well as the political skills of Charles Parnell (1846-91), the tenants were enabled to buy their farms. The landlords were given cash for their land, the tenants repaying the purchase price to the Government over a long period of time. In this poem Yeats reflects upon the effect of a reduction of rents made by the courts upon the Gregorys' Coole Park and the Gregorys' life based upon the estate.

NOTES AND GLOSSARY:

How should . . . this house: in a prose draft for the poem Yeats wrote 'How should the world gain if this house failed, even though a hundred little houses were the better for it, for here power has gone forth, or lingered giving energy, precision; it gives to a far people beneficent rule; and still under its roof loving intellect is sweetened by old memories of its descents from far off; how should the world be better if the wren's nest flourish and the eagle's house is scattered?'

lidless eye . . . loves the sun: this refers to a belief that only an eagle can stare into the sun without blinking

eagle thoughts: the eagle symbolises an active, objective person

Mean roof-trees: of the cottages whose inhabitants would benefit from having to pay lowered rents

govern men: a reference to Sir William Gregory (1817-92), the husband of Yeats's friend Lady Gregory (1852-1932), playwright, translator and co-founder of the Abbey Theatre. Sir William was governor of Ceylon (1872-7)

a written speech: a compliment to Lady Gregory, particularly for her books of Irish legends and her translations of Irish tales, *Cuchulain of Muirthemne* (1902) and *Gods and Fighting Men* (1904).

Poems from *Responsibilities* (1914)

Some of the poems in this volume record Yeats's disillusionment with Irish politicians, patrons and people; he now writes in passionate public speech, satirically and bitterly recording how his hopes for a regenerated Ireland were disappointed. Disappointed, too, were his hopes for a happy life with Maud Gonne, but his love poems, while they record the past, the old memories of her, with compassion and acceptance, still reveal how moved he was by her beauty and her regard for the people, who had turned on her. He records his delight in the achievement of art when it was fostered by enlightened and imaginative Italian patrons in the Renaissance. He rejects those who echoed the Celtic Twilight poetry he had written before the turn of the century, and he writes some superb poems out of his own emotional experiences, such as 'The Cold Heaven'.

'Introductory Rhymes'

This is a poem probably written in 1913 and first published in 1916. In it Yeats celebrates his 'old fathers', his ancestors. It was prompted by malicious remarks about Yeats and his family made by George Moore, the Irish novelist, in an article in the *English Review* in January and February 1914.

NOTES AND GLOSSARY:

Old Dublin merchant . . . ten and four: probably Benjamin Yeats, grandson of Jervis Yeats (*d.* 1712), a Dublin linen merchant of Yorkshire stock, the first Yeats to settle in Ireland. Benjamin Yeats (1750-95), Yeats's great-great-grandfather, was also a Dublin linen merchant like his father and grandfather: he had the privilege of being allowed a discount on the excise of ten per cent on wine and tobacco and six per cent on other goods. Yeats's note of 1914 states that he could not correct his 'free of the ten and four' without 'more rewriting than I have a mind for'

Galway . . . into Spain: there was a good deal of trade between Galway in the west of Ireland and Spain in the eighteenth and nineteenth centuries

Old country scholar: Rev. John Yeats (1774-1846), Rector of Drumcliff, County Sligo, from 1805 to his death, the poet's grandfather. He was a friend of Robert Emmet (1778-1803) who led a rebellion in 1803 and was publicly executed in Dublin

Merchant and scholar: Benjamin Yeats and the Rev. John Yeats

huckster's: as opposed to those of the merchant and scholar

A Butler or an Armstrong: Benjamin Yeats married Mary Butler in 1773, and the family prided themselves on this link with the distinguished Irish Butler family; the Dukes of Ormonde descended from Prince John's butler. The Rev. William Butler Yeats (1806-62), the poet's grandfather, married June Grace Corbet, whose mother's family, the Armstrongs, had military traditions

Boyne . . . James . . . the Dutchman: James II was defeated at the Battle of the Boyne (1690) by William of Orange (William III, 1650-1762)

Old merchant skipper: William Middleton (1770-1832) of Sligo, the poet's maternal great-grandfather,. who had a depot in the Channel Isles, and traded between Sligo and the Iberian peninsula

silent and fierce old man: William Pollexfen (1811-92), the poet's maternal grandfather, a retired sea captain and head of the firm of Middleton and Pollexfen, Sligo

a barren passion's sake: Yeat's unrequited love for Maud Gonne

close on forty-nine: the poem was published on May 1914; Yeats was born on 13 June 1865

'To a Wealthy Man who promised a Second Subscription to the Dublin Municipal Gallery if it were proved the People wanted Pictures'

The poem, first published in the *Irish Times* on 13 January 1913, contrasts the behaviour of contemporary Irish patrons with those of the Italian Renaissance. Sir Hugh Lane, nephew of Yeats's friend Lady Gregory, had offered his valuable collection of French impressionist paintings to Dublin on condition they should be properly housed. He favoured a bridge site over the River Liffey designed by the famous English architect Sir Edwin Lutyens (1869-1944). In disgust at the reaction of Dublin Corporation to his proposed gift he placed the pictures in the National Gallery, London, and left them in his will to London. However, he added a pencilled codicil to his will leaving the pictures to Dublin, before embarking on the *Lusitania* bound for New York; the ship was torpedoed by a German submarine and he went down with it. The codicil was not properly witnessed and the pictures were retained in the Tate Gallery, London, until 1959 when a compromise agreement was reached by the British and Irish Governments; the pictures are now shared between London and Dublin.

NOTES AND GLOSSARY:

You: Lord Ardilaun, who thought private patrons should contribute to the cost of the proposed gallery if there was a public demand

Paudeen's . . . Biddy's: diminutive of Padraig (Patrick) and pet name of Bridget; both are used contemptuously here

some . . . evidence: see note on 'You' above

blind and ignorant town: Dublin – and those of its newspapers which had attacked Lane's offer

Duke Ercole: Duke Ercole d'Este (1431-1505), the Duke of Ferrara, known for the brilliance of his court in art and letters. Yeats read of him in Castiglione's *The Book of the Courtier*, in Hoby's translation and in Opdycke's. In 1907 Yeats first visited Italy and saw Ferrara and Urbino

his Plautus: the Duke, who was a patron of the theatre, had five plays of the Latin comic dramatist Plautus (*c*250-184BC) performed at his son's wedding in 1502

Guidobaldo: Guidobaldo di Montefeltro (1472-1508), the Duke of Urbino

That grammar school of courtesies . . . Urbino's . . . hill: the refinement of his court at Urbino, situated on the slopes of the Apennines, and the good manners of his courtiers were praised by Castiglione in *The Book of the Courtier*

they drove out Cosimo: Cosimo de Medici (1389-1464), the banker, statesman, and patron of the arts who established the power of the Medici family in Florence. He was exiled to Venice in 1433, but returned to Florence within a year

Michelozzo's . . . plan . . . San Marco library: Michelozzo de Bartolommeo (1396-1472), an architect who went to Venice with Cosimo de Medici, for whom he designed the Library of St Mark's, Florence and other buildings

'September 1913'

This poem, first published in September 1913, was also provoked by correspondence in the Irish papers over the proposed Lane Gallery.

NOTES AND GLOSSARY:

you: the Irish people, particularly the newly prosperous middle-class Catholics

O'Leary: John O'Leary (1830-1907) who had introduced Yeats to Irish writing in translation after he returned from Paris to Dublin in 1885; having spent five years of a twenty-year gaol sentence for his part in the Fenian movement, he was released on condition he spent the next fifteen years out of Ireland. He was a dignified and well-read man who fitted Yeats's concepts of a romantic, idealistic nationalism

the wild geese: the Irishmen who left Ireland (largely as a result of the Penal laws passed after 1691 which, among other prohibitions, debarred Catholic Irishmen from holding commissions in the British Army), to serve in the armies of Austria, France and Spain. About 120,000 'wild geese' are reputed to have left Ireland between 1690 and 1730

Edward Fitzgerald . . . Robert Emmet . . . Wolfe Tone: Lord Edward Fitzgerald (1763-98) who served in America, became an Irish MP and was president of the military committee of the United Irishmen. He died of wounds he received while being arrested. Robert Emmet who led an abortive rebellion in 1803, was tried for high treason and hanged publicly in Dublin. Theobald Wolfe Tone (1763-

98) founded the United Irish Club, left Ireland,
went to France from the United States, became a
chef-de-brigade and led a French force to Ireland.
He was captured at Lough Swilly and sentenced to
death but committed suicide in prison

'To a Shade'

This poem, first published in 1913, is another expression of
discouragement, reflecting upon the reaction to the Irish public to
Lane's offer of his pictures to Dublin, and possibly influenced by
Swift's poetry. It links the treatment of Lane with that accorded earlier
to the Irish political leader Parnell, and to Synge over *The Playboy of
the Western World*: these were the two earlier controversies that had
stirred Yeats's imagination.

NOTES AND GLOSSARY:

Title 'To a Shade': Yeats is addressing the ghost of Charles Stewart
Parnell, head of the Irish party at Westminster who
was repudiated by Gladstone, the Irish hierarchy
and the Irish party after having been named as co-
respondent in the divorce case brought by Captain
O'Shea against his wife

monument: at the north end of O'Connell Street, Dublin

gaunt houses: of Dublin

they: the Irish people and their leaders

A man: Sir Hugh Lane. See 'To a Wealthy Man . . . Pictures'

Your enemy: William Martin Murphy (1844-1919), the
proprietor of two Dublin papers, *The Irish
Independent* and the *Evening Herald*. He opposed
the Lane benefaction; he had earlier opposed
Parnell and supported Tim Healy who led the
attack on him

set/The pack: probably a reference to the influence wielded by
Murphy's two papers. It may reflect a phrase of
Goethe's, quoted during the controversy over
Parnell's grave, comparing the Irish to a pack of
hounds 'always dragging down some noble stag'

Glasnevin coverlet: Glasnevin cemetery north of Dublin, where
Parnell is buried

'A Coat'

This poem, first published in 1912, marks Yeats's full renunciation of
his early Celtic Twilight style.

NOTES AND GLOSSARY:

I made my song a coat: I made a coat for my song

old mythologies: the Irish legends and tales he had read in nineteenth-century translations such as those of O'Donovan, O'Curry, O'Looney, Mangan and Ferguson

the fools: possibly a reference to the poets who had gathered round George Russell (Æ) in Dublin – notably 'Seumas O'Sullivan' – who wrote in Yeats's early Celtic twilight manner

Poems from *The Wild Swans at Coole* (1919)

The poems in this volume were mostly written between 1915 and 1918, but they are not placed in strictly chronological order in *The Wild Swans at Coole*. It contains poems which deal with the tower in the west of Ireland that Yeats bought in 1917: these poems are linked with the esoteric system of thought he was to set out in *A Vision* in 1926. They are cryptic but convince through their strength and assurance. The poet is now prepared to write on such subjects as his friends and acquaintances (in the elegy 'In Memory of Major Robert Gregory', for instance), and on the effects of age; but he is moving away from the bare poetry of, say, *The Green Helmet* and *Responsibilities*.

'The Wild Swans at Coole'

This poem, first published in 1917, records how Yeats's life has changed since he first stayed at Coole Park, County Galway, in 1897. When he first stayed there he was 'involved in a miserable love affair, that had but for one brief interruption absorbed my thoughts for years past, and would for some years yet'; now he realises romantic love cannot be rekindled.

NOTES AND GLOSSARY:

nine-and-fifty swans: there were fifty-nine of them; Yeats made a careful count

nineteenth autumn: the poem was written in 1916. Yeats regarded 1897 as a turning point in his life

The first time: he had visited Coole briefly in 1896, but first stayed there in 1897, and was to spend his summers there till his marriage. Lady Gregory's orderly household provided him with ideal conditions for writing; he benefited from the regular routine she imposed, the kindness he received there

my heart is sore . . . lover by lover . . . grown old: the swans mate for life, but in contrast, Yeats is thinking of the death of his love for Maud Gonne (and possibly thinking that Iseult Gonne, her daughter, to whom he proposed marriage in 1916 and 1917, might consider him an old man); his heart, unlike those of the swans, *has* grown old

By what lake's edge: the swans did not nest at Coole – the first time Yeats knew them to do so was thirty years after his first stay at Coole

---

'In Memory of Major Robert Gregory'

This poem, first published in 1918, had this note after the title: 'Major Robert Gregory R.F.C., M.C., Legion of Honour, was killed in action on the Italian Front, January 23, 1918.' (He was shot down in error by an Allied pilot, but this was not known until later.) This poem records other friends that were dead, and links Gregory with Thoor Ballylee, the tower at Ballylee in County Galway (near Coole Park) that Yeats bought in 1917 and lived in every summer up to 1929.

NOTES AND GLOSSARY:

almost settled: at the time Yeats wrote the poem he and his wife (he married Georgie Hyde-Lees in 1917) were living in Ballinamantane House (near the tower) which Lady Gregory had lent them

our house: Yeats called the tower Thoor (the Irish for tower is *tor/twr/tur*) Ballylee

turf: Irish word for peat, used in English speech there

Lionel Johnson: Johnson (1867-1902), whom Yeats met in 1888 or 1889, was a minor poet, a member of the Rhymers' Club which met in The Cheshire Cheese, a Fleet Street chop-house, to read and discuss their poems

courteous to the worst: Johnson was a drunkard, but impressed Yeats by his poise and learning

much falling: this may refer to Johnson's poem 'Mystic and Cavalier' describing himself as 'one of those that fall' (but it may also refer to Johnson often falling down in a drunken stupor!)

John Synge: John Millington Synge, an Irish writer, greatly impressed Yeats who wrote warm praise of his work. He first met Synge in Paris in 1896 and urged him to go to the (Irish-speaking) Aran Islands in the Atlantic Ocean, about thirty miles off County Galway, to write about the life of the islanders. Synge knew Irish and his plays *Riders to the Sea*

and *The Playboy of the Western World* are based
on his experience of the Aran Islands

dying: he suffered from Hodgkin's disease

stony place: the Aran Islands

George Pollexfen: Yeats's maternal uncle George Pollexfen (1839-1910), with whom he used to stay in Sligo when a young man, was a hypochondriac, who rode in steeple-chases in his youth, often in County Mayo, north of County Galway

opposition, square and trine: astrological terms representing heavenly bodies separated by 180°, 90° and 120° respectively. Pollexfen had become interested in symbolism, astrology and the supernatural

dear friend's dear son: Lady Gregory's son Robert (1881-1918), subject of the elegy

Our Sidney: Robert Gregory had a versatility similar to that of the Elizabethan poet Sir Philip Sidney (1554-86) who also died in action overseas. Gregory was educated at New College, Oxford and the Slade; he also worked in Paris at the atelier of Jacques Blanche, and exhibited in Chelsea in 1914. He was a good shot, a bowler, boxer and horseman; he joined the Connaught Rangers in 1915, and transferred to the Royal Flying Corps in 1916; he was awarded a Military Cross in 1917 for 'conspicuous gallantry and devotion to duty'

all things . . . loved by him: he had encouraged Yeats to buy the tower described in this stanza

he would ride: a stanza added at the request of Gregory's widow

Castle Taylor . . . Roxborough: both in County Galway; Roxborough was the seat of the Persse family where Lady Gregory, born a Persse, grew up

Esserkelly . . . Mooneen: also places in County Galway, near Andrahan

a great painter: see Colin Smythe, *Robert Gregory 1881-1918* (1981), p.10. This volume reproduces some of Gregory's work, which is not widely known

Clare rock: Clare, a county south of County Galway, has much limestone

consume . . . combustible: the imagery may have been suggested by a phrase in a letter of Henry James to Yeats. Yeats thought (see his *Autobiographies*, p.318) the image of dried straw, burning quickly, represented violent energy which consumes nervous vitality. But the fire needed for the arts had to burn slowly

'An Irish Airman foresees his Death'

This poem, first published in 1919, is about Robert Gregory (see notes above on 'In Memory of Major Robert Gregory').

NOTES AND GLOSSARY:

I know: Robert Gregory is the speaker
Those that I fight: the Germans
Those that I guard: the English or, possibly, the Italians
Kiltartan Cross: a crossroads near Robert Gregory's home, Coole Park, County Galway

'The Scholars'

This poem, first published in 1915, may reflect the influence of Ezra Pound, who acted as Yeats's secretary during part of 1913 and 1916.

NOTES AND GLOSSARY:

Catullus: the Roman love poet, Caius Valerius Catullus (?84-?54BC)

'The Fisherman'

This poem, first published in 1916, draws a contrast between Yeats's ideal Irishman and the real men of his contemporary Ireland.

NOTES AND GLOSSARY:

him: the imagined ideal man
Connemara clothes: homespun tweed. Connemara is an area in County Galway, the western part of which borders on the Atlantic
And the reality: the actual audience Yeats had met, described further in lines 13 to 24
The dead man: probably Synge
great Art beaten down: probably a reference to the reception of Synge's plays (Yeats was deeply disturbed by the riots at the performance of Synge's *The Playboy of the Western World* in 1907 and insisted on continuing to stage the play) and Lane's proposal for a gallery to house the paintings he intended to give to Dublin (see 'To a Wealthy Man . . . Pictures')
a twelvemonth since: Yeats wrote a prose draft for the poem between 18 and 25 May 1913 in the Maud Gonne Manuscript Book; the poem itself was dated 4 June 1914 in the same book
down-turn of his wrist: Yeats was himself a skilled fly fisherman

'Her Praise'

This poem, written in January 1915, is about Maud Gonne, forgotten, Yeats suggests, by educated society, but remembered by the poor.

'The People'

Another poem, written in January 1915, which discusses Maud Gonne. It records a conversation between Yeats and her in which he tells her how he might have lived in Italy writing, but has been caught up in work—'all sorts of trouble and annoyance for a mob that knows neither literature nor art' as he put in in a letter of 1901 (see Yeats, *Letters* (1954), p.356). She reproves him, saying that though the mob had turned against her (she became unpopular in Ireland when it was known that she had instituted proceedings in France for a divorce from her husband John MacBride) she never complained of the people.

NOTES AND GLOSSARY:

all that work: his work for the Irish literary movement, his political work for the 1798 Association, his work to create an Irish theatre and then, when the Abbey Theatre was established, his work as its Manager

The daily spite . . . of this unmannerly town: Dublin, known for its savage gossip. 'Daily' may suggest the Irish newspapers' treatment of Parnell and Lane; the hostile reception given to some of Yeats's and Synge's plays may also be indicated here

most defamed: possibly Yeats had in mind George Moore's malicious comments in *Hail and Farewell*

Ferrara wall . . . Urbino: Yeats had visited Ferrara and Urbino in 1907 on his first visit to Italy

the Duchess . . . dawn: here Yeats refers to Castiglione's *The Book of the Courtier*, which describes a prolonged evening's talk at Urbino that went on till dawn

my phoenix: Maud Gonne. When first published (in *Poetry Chicago* in February 1916) the poem was entitled 'The Phoenix'. Another poem about her, 'His Phoenix', written in January 1915, was included in the same number of *Poetry Chicago*

set upon me: probably a reference to Maud Gonne being hissed at in the Abbey Theatre in 1906 after her separation from her husband

After nine years: as the poem was written in 1915, it is likely Yeats was thinking back to the incident mentioned above

'Broken Dreams'

This is another poem to Maud Gonne, written in October 1915, which deals with vague memories and the hope that after death Yeats will see her as she was in youth.

'Presences'

This poem was written in November 1915; it is set in Yeats's rooms in Woburn Buildings, London. The three women of the last three lines may be, in turn, Mabel Dickinson (with whom he had an affair, broken off in 1910), Iseult Gonne and Maud Gonne.

'Ego Dominus Tuus'

This poem was written in the autumn and possibly the winter of 1915 and was first published in 1917. Its title comes from the *Vita Nuova* of the Italian poet Dante Alighieri (1265-1321). In an essay, *Per Amica Silentia Lunae*, Yeats indicated that the poet or artist has an uncomprehended strength on which to draw. He described how Dante saw the 'Lord of Terrible Aspect' in his chamber but could only understand a few of the things told him, among them 'Ego dominus tuus' [(*Latin*) I am your master] (*Mythologies*, pp.325-6). The poem is cast as a dialogue between *Hic* and *Ille* (Latin demonstrative pronouns, meaning the one and the other, or this man and that man). *Hic* presents the objective, *Ille* the subjective, and the poem is concerned with Yeats's theory of the self and the anti-self. Its meaning can be expanded by some of the contents of *Per Amica Silentia Lunae*.

NOTES AND GLOSSARY:

wind-beaten tower: the poem is set at Yeats's tower in Ballylee, County Galway

A lamp: a symbol of the search for wisdom. Compare the light in the tower in 'The Phases of the Moon' and the candle in 'Meditations in Time of Civil War II'

Michael Robartes: a character invented by Yeats. He appears in various stories in *The Secret Rose* (1897), and is a mysterious person who has travelled in the Near East; he also appears in 'The Phases of the Moon' and is part of the myth-making in the Introduction to *A Vision* (1925)

Magical shapes: in *A Vision* Robartes has traced many diagrams on the Arabian sands. He is reputed to have found in his travels an Arab tribe of Judwalis who remember the doctrine of a Christian philosopher at the court of Harun Al-Raschid, Kusta ben Luka (an actual person)

my own opposite: Yeats had developed a theory of the mask; by adopting a mask, by imagining ourselves different from what we are and attempting to assume that second self we can impose discipline, an active dramatic virtue, upon ourselves, see both his *Autobiographies*, p.503, and *Mythologies*, p.334

And I would find: *Hic*'s reply is to suggest that he prefers himself to an image of his opposite or anti-self. The 'And' is, in effect, 'But', an objection to *Ille*'s summoning his opposite

gentle, sensitive mind: Yeats saw a contrast between his own time and that of the Middle Ages and the Renaissance, when, he thought, people modelled themselves on Christ or some classic hero. Thus the modern period seemed to him critical rather than creative, because it looked at itself in a mirror rather than meditating upon a mask (or its opposite) (See his *Mythologies*, p.333)

Dante . . . the most exalted lady: Dante said he fell in love with Beatrice—'the apple on the bough', probably Beatrice Portinari (1266-90)—when he was nearly nine, and she eight years and four months old. She married Simone dei Bardi. Yeats thought Dante celebrated 'the most pure lady poet ever sung' but recorded that he had, in Boccaccio's phrase, 'room among his virtues for lechery'

Lapo and . . . Guido: probably Lapo degli Uberti (the son of Manente degli Uberti, called Farinata, Chief of the Florentine Ghibellines; a wise and brave man who died in 1264, a year before Dante was born), or, less likely, Lapo Gioanni (c1270-1330) and Guido Calvalcanti (c1230-1300), Italian poets, friends of Dante

Bedouin's . . . roof: the tent of a desert-dwelling arab

cliff: probably Petra (in Jordan), a city carved from rock

The sentimentalist . . . reality: Yeats thought that 'practical' men, who believed in money, position, marriage, activity at work or in play, were sentimentalists. No artist he had read of, or known, seemed to him a sentimentalist

Keats . . . Luxuriant song: John Keats (1795-1821) seemed to Yeats to have had a thirst for luxury which he could only satisfy by imaginary delights

'The Phases of the Moon'

This poem, closely related to 'Ego Dominus Tuus', was written in 1918, and deals with one of the major ideas later developed in *A Vision* (1925). The poem is also set beside Yeats's tower at Ballylee, County Galway.

NOTES AND GLOSSARY:

He and his friend: Yeats was imagining that Robartes and Owen Aherne, another invented character from the stories of *The Secret Rose* (1897), had quarrelled with him, an idea repeated in the Introduction to *A Vision* (1925)

Connemara cloth: see notes on 'The Fisherman'

the far tower . . . Platonist . . . Shelley's visionary prince . . . Palmer: a reference to John Milton's (1608-74) *Il Penseroso* where the speaker wants his lamp to be seen at midnight 'in some high lonely tower' where he can study Hermes Trismegistus and Plato (*c*427-*c*347BC), the Greek philosopher. Samuel Palmer (1805-81), the English artist, illustrated Milton's *Shorter Poems* (1889) and depicted this tower illuminated by a waning crescent moon. It is likely that Percy Bysshe Shelley (1792-1822) echoed Milton's lines in his own 'Prince Athanase', a character who also studies wisdom 'in a lonely tower'. Yeats referred to this image in *Autobiographies*, p.171, and in the essay 'Discoveries', *Essays and Introductions*, p.294

Pater: Walter Pater (1839-94), an English essayist and critic, known for his polished, involved prose style and his aesthetic sensibility. Yeats's own prose in the nineties was elaborate and decorative

the phases of the moon: see the diagram overleaf, 'The Great Wheel of the Lunar Phases', from *A Vision*

The full . . . crescents: the full is the fifteenth phase, in *A Vision* one of complete subjectivity and beauty. The dark is the first phase, one of complete objectivity, a supernatural incarnation. The crescents are phases two to fourteen and sixteen to twenty-eight (see diagram overleaf)

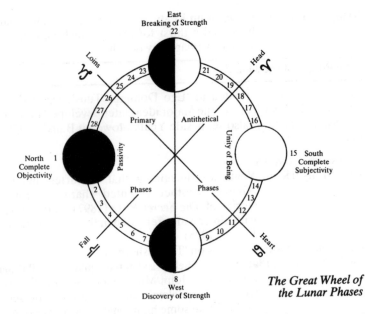

The Great Wheel of the Lunar Phases

six-and-twenty:	because the first and fifteenth phases are not phases of human life
first . . . half:	phases two to eight
towards the full:	phases nine to fourteen
cat-o'-nine-tails:	a rope whip consisting of nine knotted thongs, used to flog prisoners
Athene . . . Achilles:	an incident in Homer's *Iliad*, I, 197 or XXII, 330
Hector:	Hector, the eldest son of Priam, King of Troy, killed by Achilles in the Trojan War
Nietzsche:	Friedrich Nietzsche (1844-1900), a German philosopher interested in the idea of the superman
twice born, twice buried:	the thirteenth and fourteenth phases
the soul at war:	in *A Vision* the thirteenth phase is where 'entire sensuality is possible'—the examples given are the French poet Charles Pierre Baudelaire (1821-67), the English artist Aubrey Beardsley (1872-98) and the English minor poet Ernest Dowson (1867-1900)—and the phase is one where symbols, metaphors and images morbidly preoccupy the people of the phase
the frenzy . . . fourteenth moon:	*A Vision* gives Keats and the Italian painter Giorgione (*c* 1478-1511) as examples of the

phase, and many beautiful women who include Helen of Troy. Intellectual curiosity is not strong in such persons, nor responsibility

thought becomes an image: beings of this phase in *A Vision* have narrowed their circle of living, their efforts have ceased, their thoughts a series of separate images

Sinai's top: Mount Sinai, the peninsula at the north end of the Red Sea where Moses received the Ten Commandments (see the Bible, Exodus 19 and 20)

the man within: Yeats, in the tower

the crumbling of the moon: the sixteenth phase when there is aimless excitement, incapable idealism within such beings, examples of whom are given in *A Vision* as William Blake, the English poet, artist and engraver (1757-1827), the French satirist François Rabelais (?1494-?1553), the Italian poet Pietro Aretino (1492-1557), the Swiss-German alchemist Paracelsus (1493-1541) and some beautiful women

---

'The Double Vision of Michael Robartes'

This poem was written in 1919. For Michael Robartes see notes on 'Ego Dominus Tuus' and 'Phases of the Moon'.

NOTES AND GLOSSARY:

grey rock of Cashel: the Rock of Cashel in County Tipperary, Ireland, has several ecclesiastical ruins on it

the cold spirits: from later phases of the moon in *A Vision* (1925)

Constrained: Yeats was probably imagining here new races in a new era after Christianity, an age of irrational force (see *A Vision*, pp.213-4)

Sphinx: in Greek mythology the Sphinx was a monster with a woman's head and lion's body. Here the monster is an image of introspection, of intellect

Buddha: Gautama Siddhartha (*c*563-483BC), an Indian philosopher, founded Buddhism and was known as the Buddha. Here an image of the outward-looking mind, of the heart

a girl at play: the dancing girl is an image of art, neither wholly intellectual nor emotional but balanced between the two, combining them

Homer's Paragon: Helen of Troy, usually suggesting Maud Gonne. Compare 'No Second Troy'

Cormac's ruined house: a chapel on the Rock of Cashel restored by Cormac MacCarthy (*d*. 1138)

Poems from *Michael Robartes and the Dancer* (1921)

Some of the poems in this volume show the effect of marriage on Yeats: the playful 'Solomon and the Witch' shows how close Mrs Yeats was to Yeats's thoughts, and reflects, too, the confidence her automatic writing brought to his writing *A Vision*. 'Under Saturn' pays tribute to the wisdom that she brought to the marriage, the comfort she had made for her husband. *A Vision* provided powerful new metaphors and symbolism for Yeats's poetry, as 'Demon and Beast' and 'The Second Coming' demonstrate. The violence that followed the Easter rising in 1916, itself so precisely and poignantly recorded in the personal reaction of 'Easter 1916', continued to disturb Yeats, as 'A Prayer for my Daughter' indicates in its prayer for custom and ceremony out of which innocence and beauty are born.

'Michael Robartes and the Dancer'

This poem, written in 1919, is a dialogue, *He* and *She* representing Yeats's and Iseult Gonne's views.

NOTES AND GLOSSARY:

this altar piece: probably a painting ascribed to Paris Bordone (*c*1500-71) in the National Gallery of Ireland

Athene: Pallas Athene, in Greek mythology a virgin goddess of wisdom and practical skills

Paul Veronese: the cognomen of the Venetian painter Paolo Cagliari (1525-88)

the lagoon: at Venice

Michael Angelo's Sistine roof: Michael Angelo Buonarrote (1475-1564) painted the ceiling in the Sistine Chapel in the Vatican, 1508-12

'Morning' and his 'Night': statues by Michaelangelo in the Medici Chapel, San Lorenzo, Florence which Yeats saw on his visit there in 1907

wine and bread: a reference to the Eucharist, the Christian communion service, based on Christ's last supper when he gave the disciples the Passover bread and wine (see the Bible, Matthew 26, Mark 14, Luke 22)

'Solomon and the Witch'

This poem, written in 1918, is about Yeats and his wife.

NOTES AND GLOSSARY:
that Arab Lady: the Queen of Sheba, who came from the Yemen;

	here an image of Mrs Yeats
Solomon:	King Solomon, King of the Hebrews whom Sheba visited (see Bible, I Kings 10: 1-13); here an image for Yeats
the Fall:	the fall of man, brought about by Eve and subsequently Adam eating the forbidden fruit of the Tree of Knowledge. See the Bible, Genesis 3
Chance . . . Choice:	in a note on his play *Calvary* (1920) Yeats put into the mouth of an old Arab the idea that Chance and Choice are the first cause of the animate and inanimate world; they can only be united in God
the brigand apple:	the apple Eve ate which, in Milton's words in *Paradise Lost*, brought death into the world and all our woe
crowed it in again:	presumably the cockerel celebrated creation; he is now celebrating a perfect union

'Under Saturn'

This poem, written in 1919, describes the first visit Yeats made with his wife to Sligo.

NOTES AND GLOSSARY:

lost love:	Yeats's love for Maud Gonne
the wisdom that you brought:	possibly a reference to Mrs Yeats's share in the making of *A Vision*
an old cross Pollexfen:	Yeats's maternal grandfather, William Pollexfen, a sea captain, shipowner and merchant in Sligo. See notes on 'Introductory Rhymes', p.28
a Middleton:	one of Yeats's Middleton relatives in Sligo; his maternal grandfather William Pollexfen had married Susan Middleton, daughter of William Middleton, a sea captain and smuggler. Probably her brother William Middleton (1820-82), Yeats's great uncle, is intended here
red-haired Yeats:	Yeats's paternal grandfather, the Rev William Butler Yeats, a rector in County Down

'Easter 1916'

This poem was written in September 1916, when Yeats was staying with Maud Gonne MacBride at Les Mouettes, Calvados. In it he records his reactions to the Easter Rising in Dublin, when the centre of Dublin was occupied on 24 April by a force of about seven hundred members of the Irish Republican Brotherhood, led by Patrick Pearse, and members of the Citizen Army, led by James Connolly. They held

out until 29 April; fifteen of their leaders were sentenced by courts
martial and executed between 3 and 12 May. Yeats felt that the work of
years—the bringing together of different classes, the freeing of Irish
literature from politics—had been overturned by the violence, and he
was 'very despondent about the future'.

NOTES AND GLOSSARY:

I have met them: Irish revolutionaries, before the Easter Rising

houses: many houses in Dublin were built of granite or limestone

the club: probably the Arts Club in Dublin, of which Yeats was a founder member

That woman's days: she was Constance Gore-Booth (1868-1927) of Lissadell, County Sligo, who married Count Casimir Markievicz. She took part in the Rising, but her sentence of death was commuted to penal servitude for life; she was released in an amnesty in 1917

young and beautiful: Yeats first met her and her sister in 1894. See 'In Memory of Eva Gore-Booth and Con Markiewicz' and 'On a Political Prisoner'

This man: Patrick Pearse (1879-1916). A member of the Irish bar, he founded St Enda's School for Boys, wrote propaganda poetry, edited *An Claidheamh Soluis* (*The Sword of Light*), and was Commandant General and president of the provisional government in Easter week; he surrendered in the Post Office

This other: Thomas MacDonagh (1878-1916) a poet, dramatist, critic, and university lecturer, author of *Literature in Ireland* (1916)

This other man: John MacBride, Maud Gonne's husband, who had earlier fought in South Africa with the Boers against the British

most bitter wrong: to Maud Gonne. The most unpleasant circumstances which led Maud Gonne to seek a divorce from him are told in Nancy Cardozo, *Maud Gonne Lucky Eyes and a High Heart* (1979)

stone: a symbol for those who devoted themselves to a cause, particularly a political cause, and become bitter and inhuman as a result

a stone of the heart: probably a reference to the effect of revolutionary politics on Maud Gonne

needless death . . . keep faith: at first the Rising was not popular in

Ireland. The Bill for Home Rule had received the Royal assent in 1914 but was suspended, the English government promising to put it into force after the war was over. In the 1914-18 war approximately 100,000 Irishmen were serving in the British forces

Connolly: James Connolly (1870-1916), a trade union organiser and author, who organised the Citizen Army, was Commandant in the Post Office in the Rising, and Military Commander of the Republican forces in Dublin. He too was executed

green: the Irish national colour

a terrible beauty: the phrase implies that the martyrdom of the leaders shot by the British had altered everything and made a new Ireland inevitable

---

'On a Political Prisoner'

This poem was written in January 1919 and is about Constance Markievicz (see notes on 'Easter 1916'), then imprisoned in Holloway Gaol, London.

NOTES AND GLOSSARY:
Under Ben Bulben: a mountain north of Sligo

'Towards Break of Day'

This poem, which records two dreams, dreamed by Yeats and his wife on the same night when they were staying at the Powerscourt Arms Hotel, in Enniskerry, County Wicklow, was written in January 1919.

NOTES AND GLOSSARY:
A waterfall: probably the waterfall which falls into the lake at Glencar, County Sligo

The marvellous stag of Arthur: according to Mrs Yeats this was the stag in Malory's *Le Morte d'Arthur*, III.v. It appeared at the marriage feast of Arthur (the mythical king of Britain) and Guinevere, pursued by a white brachet (bitch hound) and thirty couples of hounds

---

'Demon and Beast'

This poem, a description of the sensation of momentary blessedness, was written in November 1918, and is set in St Stephen's Green, Dublin. At the time Yeats and his wife were renting Maud Gonne's house there, number 73.

NOTES AND GLOSSARY:

That crafty demon . . . beast: possibly, Peter Ure suggested in 'Yeats's "Demon and Beast"', *Irish Writing*, 31, 1935, the demon of hatred and the beast of desire

perned in the gyre: to pern is to move with a circular spinning motion. Yeats used a gyre as an illustration of the movement of civilisations (see 'The Second Coming' and 'The Gyres'); it can be described as the increasing spiral that can be traced conically, starting from a point and eventually expanding to a circle

Luke Wadding's portrait: a portrait by José Ribera (1588-1652) of an Irish Franciscan who became President of the Irish College at Salamanca in Spain, and founded the College of St Isidore at Rome where he died in 1657

the Ormondes: portraits in the National Gallery, Dublin, of titled members of the Butler family with which the Yeats family was connected. See 'Introductory Rhymes'

Strafford: Sir Thomas Wentworth, 1st Earl of Strafford (1593-1641), Lord Deputy of Ireland from 1632 to 1638; the portrait is also in the National Gallery

the Gallery: the National Gallery of Ireland, Dublin

the little lake: in St Stephen's Green, Dublin

green-pated bird: a duck

barren Thebaid: an area around Thebes in upper Egypt

Mareotic sea: a region in Egypt where monasticism flourished

Anthony: St Anthony of Coma (?240-345)

twice a thousand more: St Anthony, known for his enthusiasm, had a considerable effect on the spread of monasticism

Starved: probably Yeats derived this from the account of fasting given in J. D. Hannay's books *The Spirit and Origin of Christian Monasticism* (1903) and *The Wisdom of the Desert* (1904)

'The Second Coming'

This poem was written in January 1919; now one of the most quoted of Yeats's poems (especially lines 3-8), it expresses his sense of horror at what might happen to our civilisation. Here he uses his symbol of the gyres to great effect: when a civilisation has reached its fullest achievement (represented by the circle) an annunciation occurs, the arrival of a new god, at the point in the middle of the circle, the beginning of the reversal of all that has been achieved (which is symbolised by the circle's expansion). To achieve horror he uses

Christian imagery: the Second Coming is not, however, that which Christians might expect, but the antithesis of all that has succeeded, been built upon the birth of Christ in Bethlehem, his life and death. The succession of civilisations is discussed in *A Vision* (p.183).

NOTES AND GLOSSARY:

The falcon: it is tracing out a gyre as it ascends in widening circles: it may represent Christian civilisation moving further away from Christ (the falconer)

the Second Coming: see the Bible for Christ's prediction of this in Matthew 24: 1-31 and St John's descriptions of the beast of the Apocalypse in Revelations

Spiritus Mundi: (*Latin*) the spirit of the world; Yeats glossed it as 'a general storehouse of images which have ceased to be a property of any personality or spirit'

A shape . . . lion body . . . man: probably the brazen-winged beast Yeats imagined (and described in the Introduction to his play *Resurrection*) as associated with 'laughing, ecstatic destruction'

twenty centuries: Yeats thought the Christian era, like the preceding age, was likely to be two thousand years in extent

rocking cradle: Christ's birth in Bethlehem ushered in the Christian period of history

---

'A Prayer for my Daughter'

This poem was written between February and June 1919 for Anne Butler Yeats, the poet's first child, born in Dublin on 26 February 1919. It was completed at the poet's tower at Ballylee, County Galway where it is set.

NOTES AND GLOSSARY:

Gregory's wood: Coole Park, the Gregorys' estate, was near by

the bridge: it crossed the stream which ran against one wall of the tower

Helen . . . a fool: Helen of Troy, who ran away from her husband Menelaus, King of Sparta, with Paris, one of the sons of Priam, King of Troy. Yeats may be thinking of Maud Gonne (with whom the Helen symbol is associated) and her unfortunate marriage to John MacBride

that great Queen: Aphrodite, the Greek goddess of love, who was born of the foam (Greek *aphros* means foam) and thus was 'fatherless': she married Hephaestus, the lame smith and god of fire. It was she to whom Paris gave the apple when he was asked to choose

between the three goddesses, Hera, Athena and
Aphrodite. She had promised him the love of the
most beautiful woman in the world (Helen)

the Horn of Plenty: (*late Latin*, cornucopia) in Greek legend
Amalthea, the goat that suckled Zeus, chief of the
Olympian gods. Zeus gave her a cornucopia: her
horns flowed with nectar and ambrosia; the
cornucopia was a magical possession, allowing its
owner to get anything he wanted out of it

For beauty's very self: probably a reference to Maud Gonne

a poor man: Yeats himself

a glad kindness: a reference to Mrs Yeats

Prosper but little: both Maud Gonne and Constance Markievicz had
recently been in prison

An intellectual hatred: this stanza refers to Maud Gonne ('the loveliest
woman born') and her obsession with politics

Poems from *The Tower* (1928)

These poems reflect the complexity and the success of Yeats's life in
the nineteen-twenties—marriage, children, a fine house in Merrion
Square in Dublin, the tower in the west of Ireland for the summers
were the domestic basis for his public successes, which included
winning the Nobel Prize for literature and becoming a senator of the
Irish Free State. There was bitterness in evidence, too, raging at the
coming of age and apprehension at the increase of violence in the
world and the likelihood of ruin and decay. The poems show us Yeats
writing freely about history and politics, about philosophy, friendship
and love. Behind them was the structure of *A Vision*, completed in
1925, published in 1926; and Yeats now saw himself as part of the
Anglo-Irish tradition, echoing the outspokenness of, in particular,
four earlier Irish writers: Swift and Berkeley, Goldsmith and Burke.

'Sailing to Byzantium'

This poem, written in 1926, is typical of many of the poems of Yeats's
maturity in its treatment of the effects of old age, its attempts to
remedy them by contemplation of an idealised Byzantium. A
companion poem 'Byzantium' was written in 1930; see notes on it,
pp. 70-1. Yeats had read about Byzantium in several books, among
them Edward Gibbon, *The Decline and Fall of the Roman Empire*,
W. G. Holmes, *The Age of Justinian and Theodora* (1905) and O. M.
Dalton, *Byzantine Art and Archaeology* (1923). The symbolic meaning
he attached to the city was made clear in *A Vision* where he selected
the period in the city's history 'a little before Justinian opened St

Sophia and closed the Academy of Plato'; he thought that in that period 'religious, aesthetic and practical life, were one', that architect and artificers (it was a great age of building in Byzantium) spoke to the multitude and the few alike, that 'the painter, the mosaic worker, the worker in gold and silver, the illuminator of sacred books, were almost unpersonal, almost perhaps without the consciousness of individual design, absorbed in their subject matter and that the vision of a whole people' (see *A Vision* (1937), pp.279-80). Yeats had admired the magnificent mosaics with their frieze of virgins and martyrs at Ravenna during his visit to Italy in 1907; when recovering from illness in 1924 he had gone to Sicily where he saw the Byzantine mosaics at Monreale and Palermo. And he regarded Byzantium in the eighth century as the centre of European civilisation and the source of its spiritual philosophy. He had put some of his thoughts about, in the Irish phrase, 'making his soul' (or preparing for death) into 'Sailing to Byzantium', symbolising the search for the spiritual by a voyage to that city (see A. Norman Jeffares, *A New Commentary on the Poems of W. B. Yeats* (1984), pp.211-16). You should notice the link between 'Whatever is begotten, born, and dies' in the first stanza, the sensual cycle of nature, and the bird in the fourth stanza which is outside the cycle of time, of 'what is past, or passing, or to come'.

NOTES AND GLOSSARY:

That . . . country: Ireland

salmon-falls . . . mackerel-crowded: images of vigour and profusion. Yeats delighted in salmon leaping upstream to spawn (in Irish legend the hero Cuchulain was famed for his 'salmon-leap'), and he had seen the mackerel 'coming in' on the western shores of Ireland in shoals

sages: the martyrs in mosaic in the frieze at S. Apollinare Nuovo at Ravenna, Italy

perne in a gyre: see notes on 'Demon and Beast' above

such a form: Yeats's own note described how he had read 'somewhere' that there was a tree made of gold and silver in Byzantium and artificial birds that sang. Yeats was probably remembering the cover of a volume of fairy tales by Hans Andersen, on which the Emperor and his court are listening to the artificial bird. He may have been reminded of this when he was told (in about 1910) of a passage in the chronicle of Liutprand of Cremona which described the artificial singing bird in the Imperial palace

'The Tower'

This poem was written in 1925 when Yeats was sixty. The first section suggests that now his body is ageing his attention should turn to philosophy. The second lists people connected with the tower or its neighbourhood and wonders whether they, too, resented the coming of age. The third section declares his faith in poets' memories rather than philosophers' thoughts.

NOTES AND GLOSSARY:

Section I

Ben Bulben: a mountain to the north of Sligo

Plato: Yeats began to read him, probably in Thomas Taylor's translation of 1804, in the eighteen-nineties. Plato (*c*427-348BC), pupil and admirer of Socrates, taught in the Academy at Athens where he composed his Dialogues in some of which Socrates figures. Plato accepted the possibility of a common good; he thought man could only make the best of himself in a well-ordered state. His doctrine of ideas implied that what we consider actual things are not real but 'copy' real ideas or forms and thus have an incalculable element not present in real being which is free from imperfection

Plotinus: the Greek Neo-Platonic philosopher (?203-62BC). Yeats particularly admired Stephen MacKenna's 5-volume translation (1917-30) of Plotinus, though he probably first read him in Thomas Taylor's translations, the *Five Books of Plotinus* (1794) and the *Select Works of Plotinus* (1895)

Section II

the battlements: of Yeats's tower

Mrs. French: she lived at Peterswell nearby in the eighteenth century; Yeats read of the incident of the cutting of the farmer's ears in Sir Jonah Barrington's (1760-1834) *Recollections of His Own Time* (1918). See also his *Personal Sketches of His Own Times* (1827-33), pp.26-7

Some few . . . A peasant girl . . . a song: Mary Hynes, about whom Yeats wrote an essay, 'Dust hath closed Helen's Eye', in 1900; she had died at Ballylee sixty years before and he heard of her from several old people who lived in the neighbourhood. The song was written by Antony Raftery (1784-1834), the blind Irish poet, and was quoted by Yeats in his essay (see his *Mythologies*, pp.24-5)

that rocky place: Ballylee is in an area of limestone

fair: a local market

drowned: Yeats was told this by an old weaver

Cloone: near Gort, County Galway

the man . . . Homer: the Irish poet Raftery and the Greek poet Homer were blind; each sang of a beautiful woman who was praised for her beauty by the old (the old men and women who remembered Mary Hynes had seemed to Yeats, remembering an incident in Homer's *Iliad*, to speak of her 'as the old men upon the wall of Troy spoke of Helen'). Helen acts as a link between the poets Raftery and Homer and Yeats himself who compared Maud Gonne to her

Hanrahan: a character Yeats invented in the stories of *The Secret Rose* (1897) and *Stories of Red Hanrahan* (1904). He was a country poet, probably modelled upon the Irish poet Eoghan Ruadh O Suileabhan. This stanza and the next two retell the story 'Red Hanrahan' from Yeats's *The Secret Rose*

bawn: possibly a misprint for barn: bawn means a fortified enclosure, a building

a man . . . An ancient bankrupt: this owner of the tower lived about a hundred years earlier, but the dates are uncertain

dog's day: possibly an echo of Shakespeare, *Hamlet*, V.1.299, 'dog will have his day' or of the French poet Paul Fort, translated by Yeats's father's friend Professor York Powell: 'The dog must have his day', quoted by Yeats in *Essays and Introductions*, p.498

certain men-at-arms: ghosts, who had been seen playing dice in the room used as Yeats's bedroom in the tower

the Great Memory: a stock of archetypal images

half-mounted man: the bankrupt owner; the phrase implies he was not a gentleman, and probably comes from Sir Jonah Barrington

rambling celebrant: Raftery, an itinerant Irish poet

The red man: Red Hanrahan

an ear: the line is a pun, implying Mrs French was naturally musical as well as referring to Dennis Bodkin, the unfortunate farmer whose ears were cut off

The man drowned: the farmer who fell into Cloone Bog on his way to see Mary Hynes

Old lecher: Hanrahan

woman lost: Maud Gonne

Section III

Burke: Edmund Burke (1729-97), the Irish political philosopher, politician and orator. A member of the Westminster parliament, he advocated the causes of the Americans and the Irish Catholics; he impeached Warren Hastings for his conduct of affairs in India, attacked the excesses of the French Revolution, formulated conservative principles and advocated the abolition of the slave trade

Grattan: Henry Grattan (1746-1820), an Irish orator and MP in the Dublin parliament. In 1782 he carried an address demanding legislative independence for Ireland (that is, freedom from the Westminster parliament's decisions); the successful parliament known as 'Grattan's Parliament' sat during a brief period of prosperity in Ireland, but Grattan was unable to persuade his fellow Irish MPs to treat their Catholic fellow countrymen more liberally and ultimately he was unable to prevent the Act of Union (which abolished the Irish parliament in Dublin and gave seats to Irish members at Westminster) being passed in 1800

the fabulous horn: the cornucopia, the Horn of Plenty; see notes on 'A Prayer for my Daughter', p.48

his last song: swan song; the 'Last reach' echoes a poem by Yeats's friend T. Sturge Moore (1870-1944), 'The Dying Swan', quoted in Yeats's notes to the poem in *Collected Poems*, p.533

Plotinus . . . Plato: see notes on section I, above, p.50

daws: jackdaws

'Meditations in Time of Civil War'

This poem is made up of seven sections which (apart from the first, written in England in 1921) were written in Ireland during the Civil War 1922-3. After the Anglo-Irish treaty was signed in London in December 1921 and accepted by the Irish parliament in January 1922 the Republicans led by Eamon de Valera (1882-1975) refused to accept it, and civil war broke out between them and the government of the new Irish Free State. In this poem Yeats contemplates the violence that went to the creation of great houses, wondering whether the greatness vanishes when the violence, the bitterness that made them, has been dissipated by a succession of owners who have grown up in the gentleness created in those who inherit such houses. He thinks of his own tower and its past and of his children; he thinks, in Section III, of the symbolism of Sato's Japanese sword and of the skills, transmitted from father to son, that made it. In Section IV he thinks of what his descendants may or may not achieve, assessing the legacy, the legend of the tower. He was worried at the time he wrote the poem about whether he should bring the children to live in Ireland where they would inherit bitterness or leave them in England where they, because of their Irish tradition and family, would be in 'an unnatural condition of mind'. Then in Section V he describes the arrival of members of the Republican and the Free State forces, envious of their youth, their activity, their apparently careless attitudes to death. The sixth section gives a brilliant portrayal of the uncertainties of civil war, with 'no clear fact to be discerned'. In the last section he contemplates images of hatred and destruction, wondering if he could have taken part 'In something that all others understand or share' but returns to his own concerns, the preoccupation with abstract ideas, with occultism, that has lasted since his youth.

NOTES AND GLOSSARY:
Section I
overflows . . . rains . . . mounts: the image is that of a fountain
Homer: see note on Section II of 'The Tower', p.51
The . . . jet: of the fountain
Juno: a garden statue of the Roman queen of the gods, probably based on a memory of the gardens of Lady Ottoline Morrell's house at Garsington, near Oxford, where Yeats had stayed as a guest
escutcheoned doors: doors with (ornamental or, possibly, heraldic) plates or shields surrounding keyholes or door handles, protecting the surface of the door
Section II
tower: this is a description of Yeats's tower, Thoor Ballylee, County Galway. It was built by the de Burgo family and was called Islandmore Castle later, in 1585
***Il Penseroso's* Platonist . . . candle:** see notes on 'The Phases of the Moon', p.39
Section III
Sato's gift: Junzo Sato (he is alive at the time of the writing of these Notes) had admired Yeats's poetry in Japan, heard him lecture at Portland, Oregon in 1920 (where Sato was studying the canning industry)

and gave the poet a present of an ancestral ceremonial sword

Chaucer . . . five hundred years: Geoffrey Chaucer lived from c1345 to 1400. The sword was made in 1420, if we go back five hundred years from 1920. But in a letter Yeats wrote to his friend Edmund Dulac on 22 March 1920 he said that it had been made '550 years ago'

Juno's peacock: the peacock was sacred to Juno, consort of Jupiter, as a symbol of immortality. No source has yet been put forward for the idea that the peacock's scream heralded the end of a civilisation

Section IV

my old fathers: presumably Yeats's father John Butler Yeats, his grandfather, the Rev. William Butler Yeats, his great-grandfather the Rev. John Yeats, all of whom were graduates of Trinity College, Dublin

a woman and a man: Yeats's children, Anne Butler Yeats (*b*. 1919) and Michael Butler Yeats (*b*. 1921)

Primum Mobile: this was part of the Ptolemaic system; it was a wheel, the motion of which was supposed to cause the nine inner spheres to revolve around the earth in twenty-four hours

an old neighbour's friendship: Lady Gregory's house and estate, Coole Park, County Galway, were within walking distance of Yeats's tower

Section V

Irregular: a member of the Irish Republican Army, which opposed the Anglo-Irish treaty and thus brought about Civil War in 1922. The Republicans blew up the bridge beside the tower in the autumn of 1922.

Falstaffian: after the fat Sir John Falstaff, Shakespeare's comic character in *Henry IV*, Part 1 and *The Merry Wives of Windsor*

Lieutenant and his men: members of the Irish Free State army, loyal to the newly established Dublin government

balls of soot: the moorhen's chickens

Section VI

Stare's Nest: stare is the west of Ireland name for a starling. One had built in a hole beside Yeats's window

We are closed in: Yeats wrote a note of explanation: 'I was in my Galway house during the first months of civil war, the railway bridges blown up and the roads blocked with stones and trees. For the first week there were no newspapers, no reliable news, we did not know who had won nor who had lost, and even after newspapers came, one never knew what was happening on the other side of the hill or of the line of trees. Ford cars passed the house from time to time with coffins standing upon end between the seats, and sometimes at night we heard an explosion, and once by day saw the smoke made by the burning of a great neighbouring house. Men must have lived so through many tumultuous centuries. One felt an overmastering desire not to grow unhappy or embittered, not to lose all sense of the beauty of nature.'

Section VII

Jacques Molay: Jacques de Molay (1244-1314) was Grand Master of the Templars, a military-monastic order which protected pilgrims on their way to the Holy Land; he was arrested in 1307 and burned in 1314

Magical unicorns: probably a reference to Gustave Moreau's (1826-98) painting *Ladies and Unicorns*, a copy of which hung on a wall of Yeats's Dublin house in 1936

Brazen hawks: they are in contrast to the previous images of the heart's fullness

---

'Nineteen Hundred and Nineteen'

This poem was written in 1919; it was prompted by incidents which occurred during the fighting between the Irish Republican Army and the British forces combined with the Irish police force in 1919.

NOTES AND GLOSSARY:

Section I

An ancient image: this was the sacred olive in the Erechtheum at Athens supposedly created by Athena: it was created by her in her rivalry with Erechtheus to become the deity of the city, he having created the spring of salt water there

Phidias: the Athenian sculptor (c490-417BC), famous for his chryselephantine statues (of gold and ivory), notably of Athena and Zeus; he designed the marble sculptures of the Parthenon

grasshoppers and bees: Yeats got the idea from the Greek historian Thucydides (c460-400BC) and possibly from the English critic Walter Pater's *Greek Studies: a series of essays* (1895)

when young: Yeats is referring to the 1880s in particular as well as to the general pre-1914 war period

no cannon: compare the Bible, Isaiah 2:4: 'they shall beat their swords into plowshares . . . nation shall not lift up sword against nation, neither shall they learn war any more.' See also Micah 4:3 and Joel 3:10

dragon-ridden . . . drunken soldiery . . . go scot-free: references to atrocities committed in County Galway by members of the Auxiliaries and the Black and Tans. These were forces specially recruited by the British Government for action in Ireland. Mrs Ellen Quinn was killed by the Black and Tans; the Loughnane brothers were murdered and their bodies mutilated

that stump . . . ironies . . . grasshoppers . . . bees: see note above

Section II

Loie Fuller's Chinese dancers: Loie Fuller (1862-1928), an American dancer, had a troupe of Japanese dancers; she utilised 'a whirl of shining draperies' manipulated on sticks, was famous for her performances at the Folies Bergere in Paris in the 1890s

Platonic year: also known as the Great Year. Yeats got his ideas of it not only from Plato, from Proclus and from Cicero, but also from Pierre Duhem, *Le Système du Monde*. Cicero's definition of the Great Year was 'when the whole of the constellations shall return to the positions from which they once set forth, thus after a long interval remaking the first map of the heavens', and in *A Vision* (1937), p. 248, Yeats speaks of all things winding up their careers and coming round again to the beginning

Section III

Some moralist or . . . poet: possibly Shelley, in *Prometheus Unbound*, II, 5, 72-4

Some Platonist: probably Thomas Taylor in *De Antro Nypharum*, where the dead are described, after passing the Styx, as being ignorant of their previous lives yet recognising natural forms and 'their pristine condition upon the earth'

Section IV

seven years ago: 1912, when the Home Rule Bill was introduced

Section V

mock at the great: probably an echo of 'Scoffers', a poem by William Blake which combines the idea of mockery with the destructive force of the wind

Section VI

Herodias' daughters: witches. Yeats wrote in a note to 'The Hosting of the Sidhe' that the Sidhe journeyed in the whirling winds that 'were called the dance of the daughters of Herodias in the Middle Ages, Herodias doubtless taking the place of some old goddess'

Robert Artisson . . . Lady Kyteler: he was an evil spirit in the fourteenth century in Kilkenny, the incubus of Dame Alice Kyteler who, it was alleged, sometimes appeared as a hairy black dog, or a cat, or an Ethiopian. She was married four times, and it was alleged she poisoned her first three husbands and deprived the fourth of his senses 'by philtres and incantations'. She was brought before an Inquisition held in 1324 by the Bishop of Ossory

---

'The Wheel'

This poem was written in the Euston Hotel in 1921 when Yeats was waiting to board the Irish mail train for Holyhead en route to Ireland.

'The New Faces'

This poem, written in 1912, was not published immediately, possibly because its reference to Lady Gregory's growing old may not have seemed tactful. She was forty-four when Yeats first met her at a party in London in 1894; he seems to have thought he first met her in 1896 when he first visited Coole Park (with its famous catalpa tree); he stayed there as a summer guest from 1897 till his marriage.

'Two Songs from a Play'

These two poems were written in 1926, though the latter stanza of II was probably written in 1930-1. The two songs are sung by the chorus of Musicians in Yeats's play *The Resurrection* (1931) which treats of Christ's first appearance to the Apostles after his crucifixion. The play expresses Yeats's myth that Christianity terminated one two-thousand-year cycle and began another.

NOTES AND GLOSSARY:

a staring virgin: this stanza draws a parallel between the myth of Dionysus, the Greek god of drink and revelry, and the death and resurrection of Christ. Dionysus was the child of a mortal, Persephone, and the immortal god Zeus. The staring (as if in a trance because the happenings are preordained) virgin is

the Greek goddess Athene who snatched the heart
of Dionysus from his body after he had been torn
to pieces by the Titans; she brought it to Zeus who
killed the Titans, swallowed the heart and begot
Dionysus again upon the mortal, Semele

the Muses . . . Magnus Annus . . . play: they treat the event as a play
because the ritual death and rebirth of the God
seems a recurring event, part of the recurring
cycles of history

Another Troy . . . Another Argo's: these lines echo the prophecy of the
Roman epic poet Virgil (70-19BC) in his fourth
Eclogue, that Virgo, daughter of Jupiter and
Themis, last to leave the Earth at the end of the
Golden Age, will return with her star, Spica,
bringing back the golden age. (This was later
sometimes called the Messianic Eclogue and held
to be a foretelling of the coming of Mary (as Virgo)
and Christ). The Eclogue prophesies a second
Troy and a second Greek attack on it, a second
Argo. The Argo was the ship in which the hero
Jason sailed on his quest for the Golden Fleece
(the second fleece to be sought by a second Jason is
Yeats's 'flashier bauble yet'). Yeats referred to the
Eclogue several times in his prose, and was aware
that Shelley had also drawn upon it in *Hellas*

The Roman Empire . . . appalled: because the Christian message
originating in the fierce virgin (Mary) and her Star
(Christ) would overthrow the Empire. Thus Yeats
is linking Athena, Astraea (the constellation
Virgo) and Mary, Spica, Dionysus and Christ

that room: the room where the last supper was eaten. See the
Bible, Matthew 26; Mark 14; and Luke 22

Galilean turbulence: because Christ began his mission in Galilee. The
'turbulence' was foretold by astronomers in
Babylon; they reduced man's status through their
scientific views; and the Christian Church,
according to Yeats, was to make man 'featureless
as clay or dust'. In the second edition of *A Vision*
(1937), pp. 273ff, he wrote that 'night will fall upon
man's wisdom now that man has been taught that
he is nothing'. The effect of Christianity, he argues
here, is to nullify the achievements of classical
civilisation, 'Platonic tolerance' and 'Doric
discipline'

'Leda and the Swan'

This sonnet was written in 1923; it deals with the union of god and mortal, with the myth of Zeus, father of the Greek gods, taking the form of a swan and impregnating the mortal Leda, the wife of Tyndareus, King of Sparta. She bore the twins Castor and Pollux, and Helen, who subsequently married Menelaus, King of Sparta and, by running away with Paris, son of Priam, King of Troy, caused the Trojan war and hence the sack of the city by the Greeks after a ten-year siege. The myth of Leda's union with Zeus seemed to Yeats when he began the poem to illustrate his idea that the effect of the French Revolution had left Europe exhausted, and that 'Nothing is now possible but some movement, or birth from above, preceded by some violent annunciation'. As he played with the metaphor of Leda and the Swan, all politics went out of it.

NOTES AND GLOSSARY:

wall . . . roof and tower: of Troy

Agamemnon dead: King of Argos, he led the Greek forces at Troy; he was the brother of Menelaus. His wife Clytemnestra was a daughter of Leda by her husband Tyndareus; while Agamemnon was at Troy she had an affair with Aegisthus, and they murdered Agamemnon on his return to Argos

'Among School Children'

This poem was written in 1926. A prose draft of it written in March 1926 read:

Topic for poem – School children and the thought that live [life] will waste them perhaps that no possible life can fulfill our dreams or even their teacher's hope. Bring in the old thought that life prepares for what never happens

The poem is written in the eight-line stanzas that Yeats often used for his meditative poetry; half-rhymes are used effectively, and the skill of Yeats in using one sentence to a stanza should be observed. The poem's problems are finally solved by contemplation of the tree with its unity, what the American critic Thomas Parkinson has called 'a world of transcendent possibilities'.

NOTES AND GLOSSARY:

the long schoolroom: Yeats had visited St Otteran's School in Waterford in February 1926: it was run on the educational principles (based on freedom from restraint, emphasising spontaneity and neatness; see line 5 of the poem) established by Professor Maria Montessori (1870-1952) and Yeats praised it in the Irish Senate

old nun: the Rev. Mother Philomena, mistress of the school

sixty-year-old . . . man: Yeats

Ledaean body: Maud Gonne's; see notes on 'Leda and the Swan'

Plato's parable: suggested, no doubt, by Yeats's thinking of the story of Leda's eggs 'from one of which came Love and from the other War' (*A Vision* (1937) p.268, heading of 'Dove or Swan'); the reference is to Plato, *Symposium*, 190

She: Maud Gonne

Quattrocento: (*Italian*) the fifteenth century; it was 'quinto-cento' in an early version of the poem, then became 'Da Vinci' (Leonardo da Vinci (1452-1519) was an Italian painter)

pretty plumage: in his youth Yeats had raven-coloured hair

Honey of generation: Yeats took this image from Porphyry's (*c*233-305AD) *On the Cave of the Nymphs*, a work which comments on the symbolism of Homer's *Odyssey*, Book 13, in which there are descriptions of bowls and works of divine workmanship in which bees placed honey. Porphyry linked the honey with the pleasure of generation and with the aquatic Nymphs

Plato . . . Aristotle . . . Pythagoras: Greek philosophers. Plato dealt with archetypal essences, ideas, individual souls, his pupil Aristotle (384-322BC) with the general ordering of facts and the state using reason as a basis for codifying, and Pythagoras (*fl.* 6th century BC) with the universe, with the transmigration of souls, and the relations of numbers

paradigm: a word used by Thomas Taylor, whose translations Yeats used, for the Platonic idea of essence

king of kings: Alexander the Great (356-323BC) who was tutored by Aristotle in every branch of human learning

golden-thighed: Yeats got the information from Taylor's translation of the *Life of Pythagoras* by Iamblichus (*c*250-338AD), a Greek philosopher born in Syria

Fingered . . . heard: Pythagoras assigned a mathematical basis not only to the universe but to musical intervals

Old clothes: Yeats wrote to Mrs Shakespear on 24 September 1926 that this 'last curse on old age' meant that 'even the greatest men are owls, scarecrows, by the time their fame has come'

the candles light: religious statues or images in churches

Presences: presumably the statues and the children known by passion, piety or affection

---

'Colonus' Praise'

This translation of a chorus in the Greek tragedy *Oedipus at Colonus* by the Athenian dramatist Sophocles (*c*495-406BC) was written in March 1927. Yeats's translation of the *Oedipus Rex* by Sophocles was first staged in December 1926 at the Abbey Theatre, Dublin, and his translation of *Oedipus at Colonus*, also at the Abbey, in September 1927. Yeats, who did not read Greek, had first become interested in translating Sophocles in 1911-12, using a crib, and Jebb's translation, as well as his friend Oliver St John Gogarty's help. For these later translations of the 1920s he used Paul Masqueray's translations of the Greek into French, which Mrs Yeats read to him.

NOTES AND GLOSSARY:

Colonus: an Attic deme or district, Colonus of the horses, a hill about a mile north of Athens, and the birthplace of Sophocles. Its name came from the fact that the god Poseidon who gave the gift of the horse to men was worshipped there

Semele's lad: Dionysus, son of the god Zeus and the mortal Semele. (See notes on 'Two Songs from a Play'.) Semele was advised by Hera, the consort of Zeus, who was in disguise, to test her lover's divinity by asking him to come to her in her true shape. Semele did so, but was killed by the fire of Zeus's thunderbolts; he put the unborn child Dionysus in his thigh, to be born at full term. Dionysus went down to Hades, brought Semele back to earth and she then became an Olympian goddess

gymnasts' garden: a grove on the banks of the river Cephisus at Athens, sacred to the hero Academus, and the site of the Academy which Plato founded in about 386BC

olive-tree . . . Athene: in Greek myth Athena, the patron goddess of Athens, gave the olive as a gift to man during a struggle with Poseidon (see note on 'Colonus' above) for ownership of the land in Attica which she won; the first olive grew on the Acropolis at Athens, the second at the Academy

the Great Mother: Demeter or Ceres (a corn goddess) mourning for Persephone, her daughter, carried into the underworld by Pluto (or Hades), brother of Zeus and Poseidon. Persephone was given permission to spend half the year with her mother on earth and half with Pluto. The myth is obviously a vegetation myth which is concerned with the sowing and growing of corn

'Owen Aherne and his Dancers'

This poem was written in October 1917 (the first part on 24 October, the second three days later) shortly after Yeats's marriage (on 20 October); it was not published until 1924. It records Yeats's relationship with Iseult Gonne, Maud Gonne's daughter, who proposed to Yeats at the age of fifteen. He asked her to marry him in 1916 and in 1917 when he was staying at Maud Gonne MacBride's house in France. (He had proposed—yet again—to Maud in 1916 after her husband was executed for his part in the 1916 rising; see notes on 'Easter 1916', p.44). In September 1917 he accompanied Maud and Iseult to England, but told Iseult she must decide within a week whether or not to marry him: if she decided not to (as she did) he would marry a friend he had known for some years, Georgie Hyde-Lees.

NOTES AND GLOSSARY:
the Norman upland: Maud Gonne MacBride's house, Les Mouettes, was near Calvados, in Normandy
its love: Iseult Gonne
that young child: Iseult Gonne (1895-1954)
the woman at my side: Mrs Yeats
fifty years: he was fifty-two in 1917

Poems from 'A Man Young and Old'

These poems were written in 1926 and 1927. The first and second poems refer to Yeats's love for Maud Gonne, the third to his affair with Mrs Shakespear in 1896, the fourth to Iseult Gonne, and the sixth to Maud Gonne.

VI *His Memories*

NOTES AND GLOSSARY:
holy shows: the phrase has a pejorative meaning in Ireland
Hector: see note on 'The Phases of the Moon'
The first: possibly Maud Gonne
She: Helen of Troy

VIII *Summer and Spring*

NOTES AND GLOSSARY:

halved a soul: compare 'Among School Children', lines 13-17

'All Souls' Night'

This poem was written in November 1920 in Oxford, where Yeats and his wife were living in Broad Street, in a house since demolished.

NOTES AND GLOSSARY:

Christ Church Bell:	the famous bell of Christ Church, an Oxford College founded by Cardinal Wolsey (c1475-1530)
All Souls' Night:	usually 2 November, when members of the Roman Catholic church pray for the souls of the faithful who still remain in Purgatory
Horton's the first:	William Thomas Horton (1864-1919), a symbolic artist influenced by Blake and Beardsley; he was a friend of Yeats who wrote a preface for his *A Book of Images* (1898)
platonic love:	without any physical consummation
his lady:	Audrey Locke (1881-1916)
Florence Emery:	Mrs Florence Emery, *neé* Florence Farr (1869-1917), an independent 'New Woman', an actress friend of Yeats (and many others, including Bernard Shaw) who was interested in the occult. She joined the Order of the Golden Dawn and recited Yeats's poems to the psaltery. In 1912 she went to Ceylon to run Ramanathan College, a Buddhist institution. She died there of heart failure some months after a mastectomy had been carried out when cancer was diagnosed
some learned Indian:	probably Sir Ponnambalam Ramanathan who met her in London in 1902, and founded the college in Ceylon
MacGregor:	MacGregor (originally Samuel Liddle) Mathers (1854-1918) was a student of the occult (he is described in Yeats's *Autobiographies*, pp.182-3) who became Curator of the Horniman Museum, but lost this post after a quarrel and then lived in Paris
of late estranged:	there was a quarrel among the members of the Order of the Golden Dawn, and Mathers and his supporters were suspended in 1900 by a committee, of which Yeats was a member

Poems from *The Winding Stair and Other Poems* (1933)

The poetry of *The Winding Stair* is perhaps more personal than that of *The Tower*. There is celebration of friendships, condensation of memories, and dramatisation of the struggles between the self and the soul: the supernatural jostles with the earthy comments of Crazy Jane, and the eighteenth-century Irish writers receive noble praise. The tower is still present, and 'Byzantium' celebrates Yeats's image of the city in concentrated, rich imagery.

'In Memory of Eva Gore-Booth and Con Markiewicz'

This poem was written between September and November 1927. Constance Markievicz had died in August of that year, her sister Eva the year before. Constance and Eva Gore-Booth grew up in Lissadell, a gaunt big house in Sligo which Yeats visited in the winter of 1894-5. He had earlier known the girls as a child when living with his grandparents in Sligo. He enjoyed being a guest at Lissadell in 1894-5, as his letters record.

NOTES AND GLOSSARY:

one a gazelle: Eva (1870-1926) who wrote poetry, was interested in Neoplatonism and Indian mysticism, worked for the women's suffrage movement and became a social worker in Manchester

the older: Constance (1868-1927), who studied art in Paris, married a Polish nobleman, also an artist, Count Casimir Markievicz. They settled in Dublin and she became deeply involved in revolutionary politics, joining the Citizen Army, training the Fianna Scouts, and taking part in the 1916 rising. Her sentence of death was commuted to life imprisonment; she was released in an amnesty in 1917, was elected to Westminster but did not take her seat. She became Minister for Labour in the first Dail Eireann, and was re-elected in 1921. She was several times imprisoned (see notes on 'On a Political Prisoner'). In the Civil war she supported De Valera, and won her seat back in 1923

lonely years: she was estranged from her daughter: her husband and stepson had left Ireland; they did, however, return a few days before she died in 1927

gazebo: possibly a summer house at Lissadell, or a place to look out from, but, most likely, in the Hiberno-

English sense of the word—to make a gazebo of oneself, to look ridiculous—something of no value, a nonsense, something ridiculous

'Death'

This poem was written in September 1927; it was prompted by the assassination of Kevin O'Higgins (1892-1927), the Irish Free State's Minister of Justice (and a friend of Yeats) who was shot on his way to Mass. He had been in favour of the government's policy in the Civil War of executing anyone captured carrying arms and Yeats regarded him as the one man of strong intellect in the Free State government.

'A Dialogue of Self and Soul'

This poem was written between July and December 1927; it may have been suggested by Andrew Marvell's (1621-78) poem 'A Dialogue between the Soul and the Body' which Yeats had read in *Metaphysical Lyrics and Poems*, ed. J.J.C. Grierson (1921).

NOTES AND GLOSSARY:

winding ancient stair: in Yeats's tower
consecrated blade: the sword Junzo Sato gave Yeats. See notes on 'Meditations in Time of Civil War', pp.53-4
embroidery: the silk embroidery covering the sword
Montashigi: Bishu Osafume Montashige who lived in the period of Oei (1394-1428) in Osafume, Japan
five hundred years ago: see notes on 'Meditations in Time of Civil War', p.54
overflows . . . basin: compare the imagery in the opening stanza of 'Meditations in Time of Civil War'
blind . . . ditches: see the third stanza of the second section, and its 'blind man's ditch': the image comes from the Bible, Matthew 15:14
A proud woman: probably a reference to Maud Gonne

'Blood and the Moon'

This poem was written in August 1927; it marks Yeats's interest in the Anglo-Irish literary and political tradition which he had been exploring in the nineteen-twenties.

NOTES AND GLOSSARY:

this place: Yeats's tower, Thoor Ballylee, County Galway
cottages: rethatched by 1917 and adjoining the tower, they were used by Yeats and his wife as part of the tower's accommodation

Half dead at the top: the restoration of the tower was not completed; the flat roof concrete, the top room 'a waste room' in Yeats's words

Alexandria's: the Pharos at Alexandria, a lighthouse built c280 BC, one of the seven wonders of the world: it was destroyed by an earthquake in the fourteenth century

Babylon's: Babylon was famous for its astronomers

Shelley . . . towers: in his essay 'The Philosophy of Shelley's Poetry' Yeats described Shelley's use of towers (see also notes on 'Ego Dominus Tuus' and 'The Phases of the Moon'

this tower: Yeats's tower

ancestral: because Yeats is now discovering his intellectual ancestry in the Anglo-Irish writers whom he goes on to list: Oliver Goldsmith (1728-74); famous as the author of *The Vicar of Wakefield, She Stoops to Conquer, The Traveller* and *The Deserted Village*; 'the Dean', Jonathan Swift (1667-1745), the author of *The Battle of the Books, A Tale of A Tub,* and *Gulliver's Travels* and many poems and satirical writings, who became Dean of St Patrick's Cathedral, Dublin; George Berkeley (1685-1753), the philosopher and Bishop of Cloyne, County Cork; and Edmund Burke, the political philosopher and politician

the heart . . . breast: a reference to Swift's epitaph, written by himself in Latin, which Yeats translated as 'Savage indignation there/Cannot lacerate his breast', the Latin being *Ubi saeva Indignatio/Ulterius/Cor lacerare nequit*

the honey-pot: probably an allusion to the periodical essays written by Goldsmith in *The Bee*

the State a tree: a reference to Burke's *Reflections* (*Works*, II, 357) where he compares the state to an oak-tree that has grown through the centuries, an idea to which Yeats referred on several occasions

proved all things a dream: Berkeley was an immaterialist philosopher

pragmatical, preposterous pig of a world . . . its farrow: it has been suggested that this phrase may stem from Yeats's experience as Chairman of the Commission on Ireland's coinage, when the artist who had drawn the sow and piglets for the halfpenny was asked to alter the sow's shape to a more marketable one

Saeva indignatio: Swift's phrase; see note above on 'the heart . . .'
Seven centuries: a reference to the age of the tower; see notes on 'The Tower'
Tortoiseshell butterflies, peacock butterflies: common in Ireland; they came into the top room of the tower by the loopholes and died against the window panes
half-dead: see note on 'Half dead at the top', above

'The Seven Sages'

This poem was written in January 1931; it continues to meditate upon the four Anglo-Irish writers treated in 'Blood and the Moon', and to suggest that Yeats's ancestors must have known them. (See his *Essays*, p. 298.) For Burke, Goldsmith, Berkeley, Bishop of Cloyne, Swift, see notes on that poem. The 'Seven Sages' of the title, also known as the 'Wise Men of Greece' were: Solon of Athens (c638-559BC), whose motto was 'Know thyself'; Chilo of Sparta (d.597BC), whose motto was 'Consider the end'; Thales of Miletus (d.548BC), whose motto was 'Who hateth suretyship is sure'; Bias of Priene (fl. 6th century BC), whose known saying was 'Most men are bad'; Cleobulus of Lindos (d. 564BC) who is known for 'The Golden Mean, or, Avoid extremes'; Pittacus of Mitylene (d.570BC), whose advice was to 'Seize Time by the forelock'; and Periander of Corinth (d.585BC) who said 'Nothing is impossible to industry'.

NOTES AND GLOSSARY:
Grattan's house: Henry Grattan, Irish parliamentarian; see notes on Section III of 'The Tower'
tar-water: Berkeley was a great believer in its efficacy as a remedy
Stella: Swift's name for Esther Johnson (d. 1728), his friend from his days at Sir William Temple's house, Moor Park, in Surrey; she moved to Ireland with her friend Rebecca Dingley after Sir William's death. Swift's friendship with her lasted till her death; he wrote her many letters from London (the *Journal to Stella*) and poems on her birthdays
Whiggery: the English Whig party; representative of the great aristocratic families and the well-to-do middle class, in the nineteenth century they represented a desire for reform on the part of the manufacturers and dissenters. Yeats regarded them as materialistic. He thought his four Anglo-Irish writers hated abstraction. (See his *Essays*, pp. 350-3 and 435-6)

Whether they knew it or not: Burke and Swift were originally Whigs
Burke's great melody: a reference to his speeches on the topics of the American colonies, Ireland, the French Revolution and the impeachment of Warren Hastings for his actions in India

'Coole Park, 1929'

This poem was written in September 1928, and is a tribute to Lady Gregory's role in Ireland's cultural history, and the function of Coole Park as a place where so many outstanding people met each other. A prose draft read:

Describe house in first stanza. Here Synge came, Hugh Lane, Shaw Taylor, many names. I too in my timid youth. Coming and going like migratory birds. Then address the swallows fluttering in their dream like circles. Speak of the variety of circumstances that bring together such concords of men. Each man more than himself through whom an unknown life speaks. A circle ever returning into itself.

NOTES AND GLOSSARY:

aged woman . . . her house: Lady Gregory (1852-1932). See 'The New Faces', p.57

western: Coole Park is in County Galway, in the west of Ireland, near the Atlantic coast

Hyde: Douglas Hyde (1860-1949), poet, translator and scholar, learned Irish as a boy at Frenchpark, County Roscommon, where his father was rector of Tibohine. Educated at Trinity College, Dublin, he founded the Gaelic League in 1893, and became the first President of Ireland (1938-45). Yeats praised his work in reviews and wrote a balanced assessment of him in *Dramatis Personae, Autobiographies,* pp. 435-40

the Muses: in Greek mythology patronesses of art and science

one that ruffled . . . pose: Yeats himself who adopted a 'mask' of distant polished pose and courtesy to hide his shyness

that slow man . . . Synge: John Millington Synge. See notes on 'In Memory of Major Robert Gregory'

Shawe-Taylor . . . Lane: Lady Gregory's nephews. Shawe-Taylor (1866-1911) brought about the settlement of the Land Question by calling a conference (see Yeats's *Essays and Introductions,* pp. 343-5) at a crucial moment. For Lane see notes on 'To a Wealthy Man . . . Pictures' and 'To a Shade'

came .. swallows went: swallows spend the summer in Ireland, then fly to warmer climates in the autumn, returning in the spring

a compass-point: swallows often fly round a turning point such as a steeple or a high building

rooms and passages are gone: the Forestry Department took over the estate from Lady Gregory; she rented the house from the Department. When she died the Department sold the house and the purchaser pulled it down, largely for the value of the lead in the roof

laurelled head: Lady Gregory. Poets in Greece were presented with laurels

---

'Coole Park and Ballylee, 1931'

This poem, written in February 1931, is a more personal tribute to Lady Gregory than 'Coole Park, 1929', linking the poet and his tower at Ballylee with Lady Gregory and Coole Park, and summing up their common achievement.

NOTES AND GLOSSARY:

window-ledge: at Thoor Ballylee. See notes on 'Ego Dominus Tuus', 'The Phases of the Moon' and 'The Tower'

'dark' Raftery's: because the Irish poet Raftery was blind. See notes on 'The Tower'

'cellar': Irish *an soilear*; the river forms a deep pool not far from the tower and runs underground, the area being one of porous limestone

water . . . soul: an idea Yeats got from *The Cave of the Nymphs* by Porphyry, the Neo-Platonic philosopher; the Neo-Platonics used water as a symbol of generation

buskin: the cothurnus, or raised footwear worn by tragic actors in the Athenian theatre

mounting swan: according to Yeats, in a letter of February 1932 to his wife, 'A symbol of inspiration'

spot of ink: an allusion to a novel, *M. Tribulat Bonhomet* (1887) by the French symbolist Count Auguste de Villiers de l'Isle-Adam (1838-89) in which M. Tribulat Bonhomet is a hunter of swans, who, Yeats wrote in *Essays*, p.90, discovered 'that one spot of ink would kill a swan'.

stick: Lady Gregory was old and ill

books . . . pictures: Yeats praised the works of art accumulated in Coole Park in *Dramatis Personae* (1935) and Lady

Gregory herself described it in *Coole* (Dolmen Press edition, 1971). See also Colin Smythe, *A Guide to Coole Park, Co. Galway* (1983)

a last inheritor: because her only son Robert was killed in Italy in the first World War: see 'In Memory of Major Robert Gregory'

last romantics: see 'The Municipal Gallery Revisited', stanza VI

The book of the people: the phrase was used by the Irish poet Raftery

'Swift's Epitaph'

This poem, drafted in 1929, was completed in September 1930. It is a translation of the Latin epitaph Swift wrote for himself; the epitaph is in St Patrick's Cathedral, Dublin, of which Swift was Dean, and where he is buried.

'At Algeciras—A Meditation upon Death'

This poem, written in November 1928, reflects Yeats's thoughts while he was in Algeciras recovering from a serious illness, when a cold had developed into congestion of the lungs.

NOTES AND GLOSSARY:

Moroccan flocks . . . narrow Straits: Morocco, in North Africa across the Straits of Gibraltar, is roughly opposite Algeciras in southern Spain

Newton's metaphor: Newton modestly saw himself as 'only like a boy, playing on the seashore, and diverting myself, in now and then finding another pebble or prettier shell than ordinary, while the great ocean of truth lay all undiscovered before me'

Rosses' level shore: in County Sligo

Great Questioner: God

'Byzantium'

This poem was written in September 1930. The draft ran:

Subject for a poem. Death of a friend . . . Describe Byzantium as it is in the system [*A Vision*] towards the end of the first Christian millennium. A walking mummy. Flames at the street corners where the soul is purified, birds of hammered gold singing in the golden trees, in the harbour [dolphins] offering their backs to the wailing dead that they may carry them to Paradise

The poem should be read in conjunction with 'Sailing to Byzantium' (see notes, pp.48-9). In an essay 'Modern Ireland', published posthumously in the *Massachusetts Review*, Winter 1964, Yeats described Byzantium in his later poems as an example of magnificence, 'that city where the Saints showed their wasted forms upon a background of gold mosaic, and an artificial bird sang upon a tree of gold in the presence of the Emperor; and in one poem [Byzantium] I have pictured the ghosts swimming, mounted upon dolphins, through the sensual seas, that they may dance upon its pavements'.

NOTES AND GLOSSARY:

gong: in one of Yeats's sources, W. G. Holmes, *The Age of Justinian and Theodora*, he pencilled 'Gong' opposite a description of the 'sonorous board suspended in each porch of each church, and beaten with mallets by a deacon'. The sea of the last stanza is 'gong-tormented' possibly because the sea is sensual (endowed with sensations and feelings), and the gong reminds its hearers of death

an image: Yeats elsewhere alluded to 'the worldwide belief that the dead dream back' through the thoughts and deeds of their lives. The shade (ghost) fades out at last, but the spiritual being passes on to other states of existence

Hades' bobbin: In Greek mythology Hades or Pluto was lord of the underworld. This was probably a spirit; the image may come from the Greek philosopher Plato's myth of Er in his *Republic* (§610)

A mouth . . . breath: a ghost, which can seem to live backwards through its past existence

Miracle, bird . . . handiwork: see notes on the artificial bird of 'Sailing to Byzantium', p.49

Emperor's pavement: an open space, the Forum (known as the Pavement because of its marble floor) at Constantinople

blood-begotten spirits: ghosts of human beings

leave: after purgation

the dolphin's mire and blood: in Greek mythology dolphins carried the souls of the dead to the Islands of the Blest; Yeats read about this in Mrs Strong, *Apotheosis and the After Life* (1915)

'The Mother of God'

This poem was written in September 1913. It deals with the mystery of the union of God and mortal, the annunciation to the Virgin Mary (he was remembering Byzantine mosaics which show a line drawn from a star to her ear: 'she received the word through the ear, a star fell and a star was born'), the visit of the angels and the terrors of her love.

'Vacillation'

This poem was written in 1931-2. It explores the idea of contraries, which Yeats met in editing the English poet and artist William Blake, possibly in reading the German mystic Jakob Boehme (1575-1624). Yeats described the poem, in a letter to Mrs Shakespear written in November 1931, as a poor shadow of exciting experiences he had during two successive nights while walking after dark: the 'Autumnal image, remote, incredibly spiritual, erect delicate featured, and mixed with it the violent physical image, the black mass of Eden'.

NOTES AND GLOSSARY:

antinomies: contradictions (between conclusions which seem equally valid, necessary or reasonable)

A tree: it is described in *The Mabinogion* (1838-49), a collection of Welsh legends, translated by Lady Charlotte Guest (1812-95)

he that Attis' image hangs: Attis was a vegetation god who castrated himself when his mother Cybele, the earth mother, drove him to frenzy, and 'he' is presumably one of his priests: his devotees castrated themselves at the March festival of the God, during which the priest used to hang the God's image on the sacred pine-tree

ram them: an image Yeats took from Ben Jonson's *Poetaster*

Lethean foliage: in Greek mythology Lethe (oblivion) was a river in Hades, the underworld, and those who drank its water, souls about to be reincarnated, forgot their past lives

fortieth winter: Yeats was forty in 1905; he may be thinking of the break-up of Maud Gonne's marriage in that year, and the 'Lethean foliage' may refer to his love for her which made him forget everything else

fiftieth year: this experience (of 1915-16) is also described in Yeats's 'Anima Mundi', *Mythologies*, pp.364-5

Responsibility: Yeats felt a responsibility for his contribution to the thinking of modern Ireland and he thought back to the riots of 1897. See his *Autobiographies*, p.368, and the poem 'The Man and the Echo' for 'Things said or done'

Chou: probably Chou-Kung, a twelfth-century member of the Chinese Chou dynasty

Babylon: the capital of Mesopotamia, famous for astronomy and astrology; the Babylonian Empire lasted from c2200 to 538BC

Nineveh: the capital of the Assyrian Empire, destroyed by the Medes and Babylonians in 612BC

Isaiah's coal: this is presumably a reference to the Bible, Isaiah 6: 6-7: 'Then flew one of the seraphims unto me, having a live coal in his hand which he had taken with the tongs from off the altar; and he laid it upon my mouth and said, Lo this hath touched thy lips, and thine iniquity is taken away and thy sin purged'

Von Hügel: Baron Friedrich von Hügel (1852-1925). Yeats had been reading his *The Mystical Element in Religion as Studies in St Catherine of Genoa and her Friends* (1908)

Saint Teresa . . . Eternalised . . . mummy: St Teresa or Theresa of Avila (1515-82), a Spanish Carmelite nun. She wrote several books, including *The Way of Perfection, The Book of the Foundations* and *The Interior Castle*. Yeats wrote to Mrs Shakespear about this poem on 3 January 1932': 'I accept all the miracles. Why should not the old embalmers ['those self-made hands'] come back as ghosts and bestow upon the saint all the care once bestowed upon Rameses' (the ruler of Egypt, either Rameses II (reigned 1292-1225BC) or Rameses III (1198-1167BC); Yeats probably means the former)

the lion and the honeycomb: Yeats is thinking of the Bible, Judges 14: 5-18. Sampson, a judge of Israel, killed a lion, in whose carcase bees made honey. Sampson made a riddle out of this ('out of the strong came forth sweetness') but his Philistine wife pressed him till she got the answer and revealed it to his enemies

'Remorse for Intemperate Speech'

This poem was written in August 1931, and reflects upon political hatred.

NOTES AND GLOSSARY:

ranted . . . knave and fool: probably a description of Yeats's early work among the nationalists

hatred: Yeats thought it laid hold 'on our class' in Ireland where it found 'a more complicated and determined conscience to prey upon'

Poems from 'Words for Music Perhaps'

'For Music' was just a name for these poems, Yeats told Mrs Shakespear; no one would sing them. Crazy Jane was a character modelled upon 'Cracked Mary', an old woman who lived near Gort, County Galway, who was 'the local satirist' who had 'an amazing power of audacious speech'. The poems were written between 1926 and 1931.

Crazy Jane on God

This poem was written in July 1931; it suggests the passing nature of love and the permanence of God's knowledge.

NOTES AND GLOSSARY:

Banners . . . pass: a reference to the idea that past actions can be re-enacted. See Yeats, *Mythologies*, p.358

a house: probably a reference to an Irish countrywoman seeing the ruined castle (Castle Dargan, near Sligo) lit up. See Yeats's *Explorations*, p.369, *Autobiographies*, pp.53 and 77, and his play *Purgatory* as well as notes below on 'The Curse of Cromwell', pp.83-4.

Crazy Jane Grown Old Looks at the Dancers

This poem, written in March 1929, records a dream Yeats had on the first of that month. He wrote to Mrs Shakespear describing how 'The man was swinging around his head a weight at the end of a rope or leather thong and I knew that he did not know whether he could strike her dead or not, and both sang their love for one another. I suppose it was Blake's old thought, "sexual love is founded on spiritual hate"'.

NOTES AND GLOSSARY:

thraneen: an Irish word for a wisp of grass or hay. The phrase means 'not to care'

His Bargain

This poem was written after 29 March 1929. The lover, superior to ordinary mortals (Dan and Jerry), boasts that his love is lasting, is outside life (the thread).

NOTES AND GLOSSARY:

Plato's spindle: the distaff of Necessity in Plato's *Republic*, Book X. Necessity had three daughters, the Fates, called Lachesis, Clotho and Atropos (the first spun, the second wove and the third cut the thread of life). Lachesis gave the souls of men their destiny

Lullaby
This poem was written in March 1929; in it a mother sings to her child.

NOTES AND GLOSSARY:

Paris: one of the sons of Priam, king of Troy, who brought Helen, wife of Menelaus, King of Sparta, back to Troy with him, thus causing the Trojan War (here the 'world's alarms', perhaps)

Tristram . . . potion's work: in the *Morte d'Arthur*, a prose romance by Sir Thomas Malory (*d.*1471), Tristram, son of the King of Lyonesse, falls in love with La Beale Isoud, daughter of the King of Ireland. He kills a brother of the Queen of Ireland and returns to Cornwall, but King Mark sends him back to Ireland to arrange Isoud's marriage (to Mark). Tristram and Isoud drink a love potion unwittingly and fall irresistibly in love. They are betrayed to Mark, who eventually kills Tristram. In another version of the story Tristram sends for La Beale Isoud when he is dying in Brittany; she is to come in a ship with a white sail. He is told (by another Isoud) that the sail is black, and dies. La Beale Isoud discovers his body and dies beside it

Eurotas grassy bank: the main river in Sparta, in which Leda was bathing when Zeus saw her

the holy bird . . . Leda: Zeus in the form of a swan. See notes and glossary on 'Leda and the Swan' above, p.59.

After Long Silence
This poem was written in November 1929; it is written about Yeats and Mrs Shakespear, with whom he had an affair in 1896.

Mad as the Mist and Snow
This poem was written in February 1929. Yeats is considering whether great genius is mad. He had been ill, and could no longer spend his time 'amid masterpieces and trying to make the like' and 'gave part of every day to mere entertainment'. See *Explorations*, p.436.

NOTES AND GLOSSARY:

Horace: the Roman poet Quintus Horatius Flaccus (65-8BC)

Homer: the Greek epic poet (?*b.* between 1050-850BC), author of the *Iliad* and the *Odyssey*

Plato: the Greek philosopher, a pupil of Socrates at Athens; he taught there, then in Megara and Sicily, returning to teach in the Academy at Athens in 386BC

Tully's open page . . . Cicero: the Roman orator, author and politician, Marcus Tullius Cicero (106-43BC)

'I am of Ireland'

This poem was written in August 1929. It is founded on a fragment of an English manuscript (dating between 1300 and 1350), a lyric, possibly a dance song, which is placed in the mouth of an Irish girl.

Old Tom Again

This poem was written in October 1931. The invented character Tom appeared in 'Tom the Lunatic' and 'Tom at Cruachan', two other poems of 1931. (Tom Fool, or Tom o'Bedlam was a name applied to inmates of Bedlam, a lunatic asylum in London, and King Lear's fool was called Tom).

The Delphic Oracle upon Plotinus

This poem was written in August 1931. It is based on an oracle given to Amelius who consulted the famous oracle at Delphi to find out where the soul of Plotinus, the Neo-Platonic philosopher, had gone after his death. Yeats had been reading Stephen MacKenna's translation of Plotinus, and this poem echoes a passage from the Neo-Platonist Porphyry's (c233-304AD) life of Plotinus (whose pupil he had been) included in MacKenna's translation, pp.22-4. Yeats is here describing the Greek idea of heaven.

NOTES AND GLOSSARY:

Bland Rhadamanthus: one of the judges of souls in the underworld, 'bland' presumably because he is welcoming Plotinus

Golden Race: Aeacus, Minos and Rhadamanthus, judges of souls in the underworld; the latter two are described by Porphyry as 'great brethren of the golden race of Zeus'. They look dim to Plotinus, but had provided a shaft of light to guide him

Plato: see notes on 'Among School Children'

Minos: he was a son of Zeus and Europa

stately Pythagoras: the adjective used by MacKenna; for Pythagoras see notes on 'Among School Children'

Poems from 'A Woman Young and Old'

Father and Child

This poem was written in 1926 or 1927. It records Yeats's daughter Anne (b.1919) praising a friend, Fergus Fitzgerald.

NOTES AND GLOSSARY:

strike the board: an echo of a line in 'The Collar' by George Herbert

(1593-1633): 'I Struck the board and cry'd, No more'

Her Triumph
This poem was written in November 1929.

NOTES AND GLOSSARY:
the dragon's will . . . Saint George: see note on 'this altar piece', p. 42
pagan Perseus: in Greek legend Perseus, a son of Zeus and Danae, rescued Andromeda, daughter of Cepheus, King of Ethiopia, and Queen Cassiopea, from a dragon

Chosen
This poem was probably written early in 1920. The rhyme scheme follows that of Donne's (1572-1631) 'Nocturnal upon St Lucie's Day'.

NOTES AND GLOSSARY:
the lot . . . chosen: see note on Plato's Spindle in 'His Bargain'
Zodiac: through which the sun moves
the miraculous stream: the Milky Way
wrote . . . astrologer: Ambrosius Theodosius Macrobius, a fifth-century Neo-Platonist, in his comment on Cicero's *Scipio's Dream*
changed into a sphere: the souls of man and woman are ascending through the Zodiac. The 'whirling' of stanza 1 has become a sphere at a point where the Milky Way crosses the Zodiac

Her Vision in the Wood
This poem was written in August 1926. It is based upon the Greek legend of Adonis, a youth loved by Aphrodite, the goddess of love. He was killed by a boar, but restored to life by Persephone on condition he spent six months of the year with her, six with Aphrodite.

NOTES AND GLOSSARY:
the beast: presumably the wild boar
Quattrocento: (*Italian*) fifteenth century
Mantegna's: the Italian painter Andrea Mantegna (1431-1506) lived at Padua and later at Mantua
no . . . symbol: the body being carried in the litter is not a god or hero but her lover

From the 'Antigone'
This translation from the *Antigone* by the Greek dramatist Sophocles was made in 1927 or 1928.

NOTES AND GLOSSARY:
Parnassus: a mountain in Greece sacred to the Muses

the Empyrean: the highest part of the heavens, in Classical times thought to hold the element of fire, considered by early Christians to be the home of God and the angels

Oedipus' child: Antigone, the daughter of Oedipus (see notes on 'Colonus' Praise', p.61), committed suicide after Creon the King of Thebes had her shut up alive in a vault; his son Haemon, her lover, killed himself on her grave

Poems from *A Full Moon in March* (1935)

'Parnell's Funeral'

This poem was written in April 1933. In it Yeats considers Parnell's death as a sacrifice accepted, indeed willed by the Irish.

NOTES AND GLOSSARY:

Great Comedian's tomb: that of the Irish political leader, Daniel O'Connell (1775-1847) of whose rhetoric Yeats disapproved, thinking his humour vulgar and gregarious: he described him as a comedian in contrast to Parnell whom he saw as a tragedian. The tomb is in Glasnevin Cemetery, Dublin

a brighter star: Maud Gonne told Yeats on the evening of Parnell's funeral of the star that fell as his body was lowered into the grave

the Cretan barb: in his *Autobiographies* Yeats described seeing between sleeping and waking a vision of 'a galloping centaur and a moment later a naked woman of incredible beauty, standing upon a pedestal and shooting an arrow at a star'. He annotated this passage very fully. The woman, he said, 'was, it seems, the Mother-Goddess' pictured in Cretan coins of the fifth century BC

a beautiful . . . boy . . . pierced boy: his sacrificial death symbolised the death and resurrection of the Tree-spirit or Apollo

image of a star: he is linked with Yeats's vision

woman, the Great Mother imaging . . . heart: the priestess enacting the role of the Great Mother. Yeats's notes in *Autobiographies* refer to the Cretan Jupiter making an image of his son, placing the boy's heart in a hollowed-out part (corresponding to the location of the heart) of the figure

Sicilian coin: in his note in *Autobiographies* Yeats cited G. F.

Hill, *A Handbook of Greek and Roman coins*, p.163

strangers . . . Emmet, Fitzgerald, Tone: Irish leaders of the past, see notes on 'September 1913'

Hysterica passio: (*Latin*), from Shakespeare's *King Lear* II, 4, 57: 'Hysterica passio, down, thou climbing sorrow', meaning violence or madness

this quarry: Parnell. See notes on 'To A Shade', p.31

rhyme rats hear: probably refers to the poet Seanchan Torpest killing rats by rhyme in Gort, County Galway

de Valera: Eamon de Valera, President of Ireland (1959-1972); his sentence of death for taking part in the 1916 Rising having been commuted to life imprisonment, he later led the anti-Treaty (of 1922, which brought the Irish Free State into being) republicans in the civil war; he was President of the Fianna Fail party 1926-59

Cosgrave: William T. Cosgrave (1880-1965), First President of the Executive Council of the Irish Free State; leader of the Opposition 1932-44

O'Higgins: see note on 'Death', p.65

O'Duffy: Eoin O'Duffy (1892-1944), the head of the Garda Siochana (police) in the Irish Free State until 1933, who became Director of the Blueshirts, and a Brigadier General in the Spanish army in the Spanish Civil War to which he brought a contingent of Blueshirts

Jonathan Swift: see notes on 'Blood and the Moon' and 'The Seven Sages'

Poems from 'Supernatural Songs'

Ribh at the Tomb of Baile and Aillinn
This poem was written in July 1934. Ribh is an invented character, an old hermit who is reading his breviary at midnight upon the tomb of the long dead lovers of Irish legend, Baile and Aillinn, on the anniversary of their death, for, as Yeats wrote to Mrs Shakespear, on that night they are united above the tomb, 'their embrace being not partial but a conflagration of the whole body and so shedding the light he reads by'.

NOTES AND GLOSSARY:

me: Ribh

Baile and Aillinn . . . apple and the yew: Aengus, the Irish god of love, wished the lovers to be happy in his land among the dead, so he told each the other was dead and they died of broken hearts. They were then changed into swans linked with a golden chain. Over Baile's grass grew a yew tree, over Aillinn's a wild apple, and their love was told on boards of wood, made of yew and apple. Yeats wrote of them in 'The Withering of the Boughs' (c1900) and in *Baile and Aillinn* (1903)

There

This poem was probably written in late 1934 or early 1935. 'There' describes perfection, the rounding off, the shape of a sphere which is, in *A Vision's* language, 'sufficient to itself'.

Ribh considers Christian Love insufficient

This poem was probably written in 1934. Richard Ellmann in *The Identity of Yeats* (1954), p.283, suggests that the poem arose from Mrs Yeats's automatic writing when Yeats recorded in a journal that a 'communicator' had 'said "hate God", we must hate all ideas concerning God that we possess, that if we did not absorption in God would be impossible . . . . The soul has to enter some significant relationship with God even if this be one of hatred'.

Whence had they come?

This poem was probably written in 1934. The lovers are only a symbol of love, but the poem asks what lies behind the phenomenon of love, of religious ecstasy, and what shapes the events of history.

NOTES AND GLOSSARY:
Dramatis Personae: (*Latin*) the characters in a play
Charlemagne: Charlemagne (742-814), King of the Franks, was crowned Roman Emperor in 800

Poems from *Last Poems* (1936-9)

'The Gyres'

This poem was written between July 1936 and January 1937. It contemplates the ruin of civilisation, faces this bravely with the advice of Old Rocky Face to rejoice, and, finally, suggests that 'a kind of civilisation now unfashionable' will arise again (as is indicated in *A Vision's* use of the gyres to indicate the cyclical rise and fall of civilisation).

NOTES AND GLOSSARY:
The Gyres: see note on 'Demon and Beast', p. 46
Old Rocky Face: presumably some wise old eccentric, possibly founded on Shelley's Ahasuerus, described by

Empedocles: Yeats in *Autobiographies,* pp. 171-3, as 'Master of all human knowledge, hidden from human sight in some . . . cavern on the Mediterranean shore' the Greek philosopher (*c*490-430 BC) who believed all things (four primitive independent elements, air, water, fire and earth) were either blended by love (or affinity) or separated by hate (or antipathy). He envisaged a development of the perfect out of the imperfect, and a periodical return of things to the elemental state

Hector . . . Troy: see notes on 'The Phases of the Moon'

painted . . . tombs: probably the discoveries in Egyptian tombs

Those . . . again: this sentence is easier to understand if it is read thus: Those whom Rocky Face holds dear (lovers of horses and women) shall disinter the workman, noble and saint from marble of a broken sepulchre, or dark betwixt the polecat and the owl, or any rich, dark nothing, and all things [will] then run on that unfashionable gyre again

---

'Lapis Lazuli'

This poem was written in July 1936. It links a piece of lapis lazuli, dating from the Ch'ien Lung period (1731-95), that was given to Yeats by Harry Clifton for his seventieth birthday, with his thought that tragedy, individual and public, should be faced bravely, gaily.

NOTES AND GLOSSARY:

hysterical women: they are obsessed by fear of the coming war

nothing drastic is done: to stop the aggression of the Fascists and Nazis

Zeppelin: a German rigid-framed airship (named after the aircraft designer, Graf von Zeppelin (1838-1917); Zeppelins bombed London in the 1914-18 war

King Billy bomb-balls: an echo of 'The Battle of the Boyne', an Irish ballad. King Billy is William of Orange, who defeated James II at the Battle of the Boyne in Ireland in 1690:

> King James has pitched his tent between
> The lines for to retire
> But King William threw his bomb-balls in
> And set them all on fire

Hamlet . . . Lear . . . Ophelia . . . Cordelia: Hamlet and Ophelia are characters in Shakespeare's *Hamlet,* Lear and Cordelia in his *King Lear.* The two women are unlike the hysterical women of the first line

lines to weep: Yeats, being told of a heroine weeping at the final curtain of a play by Lady Gregory, thought this should never occur

blazing into the head: Yeats thought that Shakespearean heroes conveyed a sudden enlargement of vision, an ecstasy at the approach of death, and quoted Lady Gregory's saying: 'Tragedy must be a joy to the man who dies'. See his *Essays and Introductions*, pp. 522-3

It: tragedy wrought to its utmost

Callimachus: a late-fifth-century Greek sculptor who was known for his technical skill

lamp-chimney: he made a golden lamp for the Erechtheum in Athens which is described in Pausanias, *Description of Greece* I, 26, 6-7

Two Chinamen: this begins the description of the lapis lazuli which stood on a mantelpiece in Yeats's house

---

'An Acre of Grass'

This poem, written in November 1936, was inspired by rereading the German author Nietzsche, especially his *The Dawn of Day*.

NOTES AND GLOSSARY:

An acre: the Yeats family moved in 1932 to Riversdale, Rathfarnham, County Dublin. This was a small farmhouse, leased for thirteen years, with an orchard, lawns, flower garden and fruit garden

rag and bone: compare the 'rag-and-bone shop of the heart' in 'The Circus Animals' Desertion'

an old man's frenzy: compare 'Mad as the Mist and Snow'

Timon and Lear: the main characters in Shakespeare's *Timon of Athens* and *King Lear*

Blake: the English poet and engraver who influenced Yeats and whose *Prophetic Books* (3 vols, 1893) he edited with Edwin Ellis in 1893

Michael Angelo: see note on 'Michael Robartes and the Dancer'

'What then?'

This poem was probably written in 1936. This poem, like 'An Acre of Grass', was stimulated by a rereading of Nietzsche.

NOTES AND GLOSSARY:

school: The High School, Dublin, an Erasmus Smith foundation which Yeats from 1881 to 1883. He was earlier a pupil at the Godolphin School, Hammersmith from 1875 to 1880

Plato's ghost: see note on 'The Tower', I

small old house: Riversdale, Rathfarnham; see note on 'An Acre of Grass'

'Beautiful Lofty Things'

This poem was probably written in 1937. It consists of particular moments of memory in which the nature of the people Yeats is remembering is recaptured. They seem to him, looking back, to have been like the Olympian gods and goddesses, superior to the mundane.

NOTES AND GLOSSARY:

O'Leary's . . . head: see notes on 'September 1913'

My father . . . Abbey stage: the artist John Butler Yeats (1839-1922) who spoke at the debate in the Abbey Theatre, Dublin, held after the riots which greeted Synge's play *The Playboy of the Western World* in 1907

Standish O'Grady . . . drunken audience: O'Grady (1846-1928), an Irish novelist and historian, whose writings had a great influence on Yeats and his generation. The speech was delivered at a dinner in honour of the Irish Literary Theatre

Augusta Gregory . . . drawn up: See notes on 'The New Faces', 'Coole Park, 1929' and 'Coole Park and Ballylee, 1931'. She told a threatening tenant who wanted to take over some Coole Park land 'how easy' it would be to shoot her 'through the unshuttered window if he wanted to use violence' when she wrote letters every evening

Maud Gonne: Yeats first proposed to her at Howth in 1891

Pallas Athene: he compared her to a goddess on many occasions

Olympians: the Greek gods, who lived on Mount Olympus

'The Curse of Cromwell'

This poem was written between November 1936 and January 1937. It is meant to be spoken by a wandering peasant poet in Ireland.

NOTES AND GLOSSARY:

Cromwell's: after Charles I was executed in 1649 and the Commonwealth established, Oliver Cromwell (1599-1658) went to Ireland where he sacked Drogheda and Wexford; he left in 1650

beaten into the clay: this phrase comes from Frank O'Connor's translation 'Kilcash'. By the settlement Act of 1652 and a further act of 1653 Cromwell confiscated about eleven million out of the total of twenty million acres of Irish land, leaving Irish landowners only Connaught and Clare

his fathers . . . crucified: a line from a translation of a poem by the Irish poet Egan O'Rahilly (1670-1726)

fox . . . Spartan boy's: a story in the Life of Lycurgus (c390-c325BC) in the *Lives of the Ten Orators* tells how a Spartan boy stole a fox and when caught hid it under his clothes: he let it gnaw him to death rather than be found out to be a thief

great house . . . old ruin: see notes on 'Crazy Jane on God'

'Come gather round me, Parnellites'

This poem was written in September 1936.

NOTES AND GLOSSARY:

Parnellites . . . our chosen man: followers of Charles Stewart Parnell. See notes on 'To a Shade'

Stand . . . while you can: Parnell's followers were likely to have been old men by 1936; he died in 1891

a lass: Mrs O'Shea. Her husband Captain William Henry O'Shea brought an action for divorce, naming Parnell as co-respondent

The Bishops and the Party: Gladstone (the English prime minister whom Parnell had converted to the cause of Home Rule for Ireland) and the Irish hierarchy repudiated Parnell when the divorce case occurred, and the Irish parliamentary party (of which Parnell was leader) split

sold his wife . . . betrayed: Yeats had read Henry Harrison, *Parnell Vindicated* (1931), and wrote to Dorothy Wellesley on 8 September 1936 to say 'Mrs O'Shea was a free woman when she met Parnell, O'Shea had been paid to leave her free, and if Parnell had been able to raise £20,000 would have let himself be divorced instead of [citing] Parnell [as co-respondent]'

'The Wild Old Wicked Man'

This poem was probably written between 1937 and 1938. The 'old man' in the skies is God.

'The Pilgrim'

This poem was probably written in 1937 (possibly after Yeats visited the Municipal Gallery in August: there is a painting of the Pilgrimage there which he recorded seeing on that visit). It deals with the pilgrimage to Lough Derg, a small lake on the borders of County Donegal and County Fermanagh.

NOTES AND GLOSSARY:

Lough Derg's holy island: St Patrick is supposed to have fasted in the cave on the island, and had a vision of the next world there. There are medieval accounts of the pilgrimage and Yeats read the Spanish dramatist Calderon's (1600-81) play on the subject as well as Archdeacon Seymour's *St Patrick's Purgatory: A Medieval Pilgrimage in Ireland* (1919)

the Stations: of the Cross, usually fourteen: they depict Christ's passion and crucifixion

Purgatory: where the Soul is purified, in Catholic doctrine, before going to heaven

black . . . bird: probably a bird described in an account by Antonio Mannini, a Florentine merchant who visited the purgatory in 1411, quoted by Archdeacon Seymour, *St Patrick's Purgatory,* pp. 55-7

'The Municipal Gallery Revisited'

This poem was written between August and early September 1937. It was prompted by a visit Yeats made to the Dublin Municipal Gallery in Charlemont Square, Dublin in August 1937. 'Restored to many friends' he sat down 'after a few minutes, overwhelmed with emotion'.

NOTES AND GLOSSARY:

thirty years: he thought the pictures presented Ireland 'in spiritual freedom' and the pictures he mentions go back to the 1916 Rising, which could be taken as the creation of that freedom

An ambush: probably a painting by Sean Keating (1889-1977)

pilgrims: in *St Patrick's Purgatory* by Sir John Lavery (1856-1941)

Casement: in *The Court of Criminal Appeal* by Sir John Lavery. Sir Roger Casement (1864-1916) was a British consular official. He joined Sinn Fein in 1914, went to Germany, returned to Ireland in a

U-boat in 1916 and was arrested in south-west Ireland; he was tried on a charge of high treason in London and hanged

Griffith: Arthur Griffith (1872-1922) edited the *United Irishman* and *Sinn Fein*. Vice-president of Dail Eireann in 1918, he led the Irish plenipotentiaries who negotiated the Anglo-Irish treaty in 1921, became President of the Dail in 1922 and died that year

Kevin O'Higgins: see notes on 'Death', p. 65

revolutionary Soldier . . . Tricolour: in Lavery's painting *The Blessing of the Colours*; the soldier was a member of the Irish Free State army

woman's portrait: possibly a portrait of Lady Beresford by the American painter John Singer Sargent (1856-1925) who worked in England from 1885

Heart-smitten . . . recovering: Yeats's heart was giving him trouble at the time of the visit

Augusta Gregory's son: see notes on 'In Memory of Major Robert Gregory', pp. 33-4

her sister's son: the portrait is by Charles Shannon (1863-1937), an English painter and lithographer

Hugh Lane: see notes on 'To a wealthy Man . . . Pictures', p. 29. The portrait is probably that painted by Sargent

'onlie begetter': the phrase used in the dedication to 'Mr W.H.' in the Dedication to Shakespeare's *Sonnets*

Hazel Lavery: Sir John Lavery's second wife (*d.* 1935) whose portrait was on Irish bank notes until recently

living and dying: the first painting is 'Hazel Lavery at her Easel', the second 'The Unfinished Harmony'

Mancini's portrait: Antonio Mancini (1852-1930) was an Italian artist

Augusta Gregory: see notes on 'The New Faces', 'Coole Park, 1929' and 'Coole Park and Ballylee, 1931'

Rembrandt: the famous Dutch painter and etcher Rembrandt van Rijn (1606-69)

John Synge: see notes on 'In Memory of Major Robert Gregory'

that woman . . . that household: Lady Gregory and Coole Park

Childless: Yeats's first child, Anne Butler Yeats, was born in 1919

No fox . . . Spenser: an echo of Edmund Spenser's (?1552-99) 'The Death of the Earl of Leicester': 'He now is gone, the whiles the Foxe is crept/Into the hole, the which the badger swept'

Antaeus-like: Antaeus, son of Poseidon (god of the sea and the underworld in Greek mythology), when attacked by Hercules, got strength from his mother, Earth, whenever he touched the ground

noble and beggar-man: Lady Gregory used to quote the Greek philosopher Aristotle: 'To think like a wise man, but express oneself like the common people'

'Are you content?'

This poem was probably written late in 1937 or early in 1938. The poem could be read as an answer to 'Introductory Rhymes' of *Responsibilities* in which Yeats had lamented that he had no child, only 'a book' to link him to his ancestors. His subsequent marriage in 1917 had continued his family line; but he is still not content when he views his achievement. This poem could also be compared with 'An Acre of Grass' or 'The Man and the Echo'.

NOTES AND GLOSSARY:

son: his father John Butler Yeats; see note on 'Beautiful Lofty Things'

Grandson: either the Rev. William Butler Yeats, the 'red-headed rector', or 'Old William Pollexfen', both mentioned in the second stanza of this poem. See notes on 'Introductory Rhymes', p. 28

great-grandson: most likely the Rev. John Yeats, described in the first two lines of the second stanza; or William Pollexfen's father (details of whom are not known) or William Middleton, the 'smuggler' of the second stanza or, least likely, William Corbet (1737-1824). See notes on 'Introductory Rhymes'

He . . . cross: Rev. John Yeats, rector of Drumcliff, County Sligo. The cross is Celtic in form and stands in Drumcliff churchyard

Sandymount Corbets: Yeats's great-uncle Robert Corbet owned Sandymount Castle, south of Dublin. Yeats's father spent a lot of time there when he was an undergraduate and Yeats was born in a house nearby in 1865

Butlers far back: a reference to the wife of Benjamin Yeats: see notes on 'Introductory Rhymes'

Browning meant: a reference to *Pauline* (1833) by Robert Browning (1812-89): 'an old hunter/Talking with gods, or a high-crested chief/Sailing with troops of friends to Tenedos'

'The Statues'

This poem was written between April and June 1938. It is, broadly speaking, about the influence of art or literature on civilisation.

NOTES AND GLOSSARY:

Pythagoras: Yeats is suggesting that Pythagoras (see note on 'Among School Children', p. 60) with his theory of numbers affected Greek sculptors who carved their statues by exact measurements

Greater than Pythagoras: the Greek sculptors, not the Greek galleys that defeated the Persians at the naval battle of Salamis (480BC), really created Europe. In *On the Boiler* (1939) Yeats wrote that when 'the Doric Studios sent out those broad-backed marble statues against the multiform, vague, expressive Asiatic sea, they gave to the sexual instinct of Europe its goal, its fixed type'

Phidias: the greatest sculptor of Greece (*b.c*500BC), who was commissioned by Pericles to execute the main statues which were to adorn Athens; he built the Parthenon, the Propylaea, and himself carved the famous statue of the Athena at Athens and that of Zeus at Olympia

One image . . . tropic shade: Yeats is here referring to the effect of the Greek sculptors who followed Alexander the Great to India

No Hamlet . . . Middle Ages: the later image in this stanza of Grimalkin, a name for a cat (see Shakespeare's *Macbeth* I, 1.9,), may have suggested the common notion that cats grow thin by eating flies which was then transferred to Hamlet. The 'dreamer of the Middle Ages' appears in a passage in *Autobiographies* (pp. 141-2) which throws light on this elliptic stanza:

> . . . the broad vigorous body suggests a mind that has no need of the intellect to remain sane, though it give itself to every fantasy: the dreamer of the Middle Ages. It is . . . the resolute European image that yet half remembers Buddha's motionless meditation, and has no trait in common with the wavering lean image of hungry speculation, that cannot but because of certain famous Hamlets of our

stage fill the mind's eye. Shakespeare himself foreshadowed a symbolic change, that is a change in the whole temperament of the world, for though he called his Hamlet 'fat' and even 'scant of breath', he thrust between his fingers agile rapier and dagger

Empty eyeballs: in *A Vision* Yeats wrote that the 'Greeks painted the eyes of marble statues and made out of enamel or glass or precious stones those of their bronze statues, but the Roman was the first to drill a round hole to represent the pupil, and because, as I think, of a preoccupation with the glance characteristic of a civilisation in its final phase'

Pearse summoned Cuchulain . . . Post Office: for Pearse see note on 'Easter 1916', p. 44. Yeats remarked in a letter of 25 June 1938 to Edith Shackleton Heald that 'Pearse and some of his followers had a cult' of Cuchulain the Irish hero (Pearse was in the General Post Office in Dublin, in front of which he read the proclamation of the Irish Republic in 1916; the building was heavily shelled, and Pearse and the others who had occupied it eventually surrendered); he continued: 'The [Irish] Government has put a statue of Cuchulain in the rebuilt post office to commemorate this'

What intellect . . . measurement . . . face: Pearse is described as summoning the forces of the past into being through the images created by intellect, the Cuchulain of the Irish legends, recreated through the literary revival, and given its archaic strength by contrast with the shapelessness of modern life, its 'formless spawning fury'

'News for the Delphic Oracle'

This poem was written during 1938. It is an ironic way of presenting earlier subjects and imagery. The fairy princess Niamh, treated idealistically in Yeats's early long poem *The Wanderings of Oisin* (1889), is now summed up as a 'Man-picker'. The great dead, the immortals, are seen as golden codgers. The whole poem has an earthy vigour about it; the dolphins conveying the souls 'pitch their burdens off'; the last stanza describes a Poussin picture in earthy terms. Contrast this poem with 'The Delphic Oracle upon Plotinus' and notes on it, p. 76.

NOTES AND GLOSSARY:

codgers: a word usually used with derisive meaning for an old or eccentric man

Oisin: the son of Finn and Saeve (of the Sidhe), he spent three hundred years in three islands with Niamh in the other world in Yeats's *The Wanderings of Oisin*, which was founded on 'the Middle Irish dialogues of S. Patrick and Oisin and a certain Gaelic poem of the last century'

Pythagoras . . . choir of love: see notes on 'Among School Children', p. 60

a dolphin's back: see notes on dolphins in 'Byzantium', pp. 70-1

Innocents: possibly the Holy Innocents, children whom Herod's soldiers killed when Herod tried to eliminate Jesus. See the Bible, Matthew 2: 16-18

Peleus . . . Thetis: the stanza describes *The Marriage of Peleus and Thetis* (now entitled *Acis and Galatea*) by the French painter Caspar Poussin (1613-75) in the National Gallery of Ireland. In Greek legend Peleus married Thetis, a Nereid

Pan's cavern . . . music: Greek god of fertility, usually represented with horns on his human head, with the body of a goat from the waist down. He invented the flute and liked caverns

nymphs . . . satyrs: beautiful female nature spirits; ugly often goat-like sylvan gods who chased the nymphs

---

'Long-legged fly'

This poem was written between November 1937 and April 1938.

NOTES AND GLOSSARY:

Caesar: Caius Julius Caesar (?102-44BC) Roman general, statesman and historian

topless towers: of Troy. The phrase comes from Christopher Marlowe's (1564-93) *The Tragical History of Dr Faustus*, v.1. 90-5

She: Maud Gonne

the Pope's chapel: the Sistine Chapel in the Vatican, Rome

Michael Angelo: who painted the famous ceiling in the chapel which shows Adam about to be awakened into life by God

---

'A Bronze Head'

This poem was probably written between 1937 and 1938.

NOTES AND GLOSSARY:

entrance:	to the Municipal Gallery of Modern Art, Dublin. See 'The Municipal Gallery Revisited', p. 85
bronze head:	of Maud Gonne, by Laurence Campbell, RHA
Hysterica passio:	see notes on 'Parnell's Funeral', p. 79
tomb-haunter:	probably a reference to Maud Gonne's attending public funerals of those associated with the republican cause; she habitually dressed in long black garments and a black veil in the nineteen-twenties and thirties
McTaggart:	J. McT. E. McTaggart (1866-1925), the Cambridge philosopher

'High Talk'

This poem was written between late July and August 1938, and is probably founded on memories of circuses visiting Sligo in Yeats's youth. Compare it with 'The Circus Animals' Desertion'. The stilts may refer back to the 'stilted boys', the old Irish heroes, of 'The Circus Animals' Desertion'; their being stolen may refer to those who adopted Yeats's Celtic Twilight style, as in the poem 'A Coat'. Malachi (?Yeats) is replacing the stolen stilts, but is stalking out of the town in the cold reality of dawn light, possibly the facing of death.

NOTES AND GLOSSARY:

patching old heels: the women are patching socks in upstairs rooms
Malachi Stilt-Jack: Malachi is used as a Christian name, after the minor Hebrew prophet
sea-horses: the waves

'Why should not old men be mad?'

This poem was written in January 1936.

NOTES AND GLOSSARY:

journalist:	probably R. M. Smylie, editor of the *Irish Times* at the time; like Yeats he had Sligo connections, his father having edited a Sligo newspaper
A girl:	Iseult Gonne
a dunce:	Francis Stuart (*b.*1902), the novelist and poet, about whom Yeats had changing views. Stuart's *Black List section H* (1971) gives one account of the marriage
A Helen:	either Maud Gonne or Constance Markievicz (see notes on 'In Memory of Eva-Gore-Booth, and Con Markiewicz', p. 64)

'The Circus Animals' Desertion'

This poem was probably written between November 1937 and September 1938.

NOTES AND GLOSSARY:

Winter and summer . . . on show: this emphasises the totality of Yeats's commitment to his art, since circuses used to work a half-year season of performances

Stilted boys . . . chariot . . . Lion . . . woman: possibly the recreation of Irish legendary heroes such as Conchubar, Cuchulain, Fergus, Oisin and so on; the chariot may be Cuchulain's; the lion and woman may refer to Maud Gonne (described as 'half-lion half child' in 'Against Unworthy Praise' (a poem included in *The Green Helmet and Other Poems* (1910))

sea-rider Oisin: in Yeats's *The Wanderings of Oisin* he gallops off over the sea with Niamh

led by the nose: Oisin and his friends when hunting meet Niamh on the edge of the sea, and she has chosen Oisin and has come to invite him to mount her horse with her, to know the Danaan leisure and have her as his wife

three enchanted islands, allegorical dreams: they represent the three things man is always seeking, Yeats told his friend Katharine Tynan in a letter of 1888, 'infinite feeling, infinite battle and infinite repose' – summed up as gaiety, battle and repose in the poem

Countess Cathleen . . . gave it: the play of this title which Yeats wrote for Maud Gonne, in which she played the Countess in the first production, 8 May 1899. In the play the Countess opposes two devils who offer to buy for gold the souls of starving peasants; she sacrifices her goods to buy food and sells her own soul, to the horror of the poet Kevin

my dear: Maud Gonne

the Fool and Blind Man . . . sea: this refers to the action of Yeats's play *On Baile's Strand* (1904)

Heart-mysteries: possibly a reference to Maud Gonne's marriage

the dream itself: of an ideal love

Players . . . stage: from 1903 to 1910 Yeats acted as General Manager of the Abbey Theatre

'The Man and the Echo'

This poem was written in July 1938. It deals with death, and reaches the final admission that 'Man' simply does not know what may happen after death; he only knows that he faces the Rocky Voice.

NOTES AND GLOSSARY:

Alt: a rocky fissure on Knocknarea, County Sligo

that play: *Cathleen ni Houlihan* (1902), in which Maud Gonne played the part of Cathleen. The play had an impressive effect on its audiences. Yeats may have read Stephen Gwynn, *Irish Literature and Drama* (1936), p. 158. Gwynn attended the theatre but went home asking himself 'if such plays should be produced unless one was prepared for people to go out to shoot and be shot . . . . Miss Gonne's impersonation had stirred the audience as I have never seen another audience stirred'

woman's . . . brain: she was Margot Collis, who wrote under the name Margot Ruddock. Yeats wrote several poems about her: 'A Crazed Girl' of May 1936, 'Sweet Dancer' of January 1937, and 'Margot', published posthumously. There is an account of her madness in a letter of 22 May 1936 to Mrs Shakespear. See Yeats, *Letters* (1954), p. 856

a house: possibly Coole Park, though it might imply 'big houses' in general

bodkin: a symbol of suicide

Rocky Voice: compare this image with that of 'Old Rocky Face' in 'The Gyres'

great night: presumably of death

'Under Ben Bulben'

This poem was finished in early September 1938.

NOTES AND GLOSSARY:

sages . . . Mareotic Lake: see notes on 'Demon and Beast', p.46

Witch of Atlas: in Shelley's poem 'The Witch of Atlas' she was a symbol of the beauty of wisdom, a Naiad turned into a cloud by the embrace of the sun. She travelled along the Nile 'by Moeris and the Mareotid Lakes'

those horsemen . . . women: probably the visionary people described to

Yeats by his uncle George Pollexfen's maid Mary Battle. See notes on Pollexfen in notes on 'In Memory of Major Robert Gregory', p.34

Ben Bulben: the mountain in Sligo particularly associated with the Fianna, the mounted warriors who served Finn

Mitchel: John Mitchel (1815-75), an Irish nationalist. Transported to Australia, he wrote in November 1853 a powerful *Jail Journal* (1854) in which he, in parody of the Anglican order of Service 'Give us peace in our time, O Lord', substituted 'war' for 'peace'. He escaped from Australia to America, returning later to become an MP in Ireland

a stark Egyptian: Plotinus, born in Lycopolis, Egypt, who thought objects were themselves imitations, and that art imitated objects, thus going back to the ideas from which Nature derives

gentler Phidias: see notes on 'The Statues', p.88

Sistine Chapel . . . Adam: see notes on 'Long-legged Fly', p.90

Quattrocento: Italian word for the fifteenth century

Calvert: Edward Calvert (1799-1883), visionary artist

Wilson: Richard Wilson (1714-82), landscape painter

Blake: William Blake, English poet, painter, engraver and mystic

Claude: Claude Lorraine (1600-82), a French landscape painter

Palmer's phrase: Yeats in his essay 'Blake's illustrations to Dante' (*Essays and Introduction*, p. 125) quoted Samuel Palmer, who described Blake's illustrations (in Thornton's *Virgil*) to the first Eclogue of Virgil as being 'like all this wonderful artist's work, the drawing aside of the fleshly curtain, and the glimpse which all the most holy studious saints and sages have enjoyed, of the rest which remains to the people of God'

the lords and ladies . . . clay: from Yeats's friend the Irish author Frank O'Connor's (pseudonym of Michael O'Donovan (1903-66)) translation *Kilcash*: 'The earls, the lady, the people beaten into the clay'

Drumcliff churchyard and . . . An ancestor: Yeats arranged that he should be buried in the churchyard where his great-grandfather had been rector, on the road to Bundoran to the north of Sligo. He died at Roquebrune, France on 28 January 1939; his body was re-interred at Drumcliff on 17 September 1948

Part 3

Commentary

Subject matter

Irish legends and folktales

1. Yeats drew upon local Sligo legends and folktales which he had heard there as a child and as a young man. He collected them in *Fairy and Folk Tales of the Irish Peasantry* (1888) and in *Irish Fairy Tales* (1892), and *The Celtic Twilight* (1893) contained his own essays and some poems in this vein. This material influenced his 'Celtic Twilight' poetry, in such poems as 'The Stolen Child' and 'The Man who Dreamed of Fairyland'. He also heard fragments of songs and ballads, and 'Down by the Salley Gardens' shows how he used a song that he had heard an old woman singing in Sligo. The country people in Sligo believed in the supernatural, and many of their stories, transmitted orally, came from earlier times.

2. Yeats read widely in translations of Irish literature, since he did not himself know Irish. From these translations he learned of the two main cycles of pagan Irish tales, those of the Red Branch, or Ulster cycle, and those of the later Fenian cycle. From the former he learned of King Conor or Conchubar of Ulster, and his court, especially the hero Cuchulain, his wife Emer, his mistress Eithne Inguba and his goddess lover Fand. He knew of Conchubar's wife, Ness, who persuaded her second husband Fergus to give up his throne to Conchubar. And he knew of the warrior queen Maeve, and her husband Aillell, as well as of other warriors such as Caoilte. He was particularly interested in Cuchulain, writing about him at different stages of his career. For example, in the early period came 'Cuchulain's Fight with the Sea', in the middle the play *On Baile's Strand*, followed by *At the Hawk's Well*, and in the late the poem 'Cuchulain Comforted' and the play *The Death of Cuchulain*. He was also interested in the Deirdre legend, in which Conchubar puts Deirdre, the daughter of his harper Felimid, in the charge of a nurse, Lavarcham, intending to marry her when she was older. She, however, runs off with one of Conchubar's captains, Naoise, son of Usna, and his brothers Ainnle and Ardan, to Scotland. The lovers return under the safe conduct of Fergus, who leaves them, because

of *geasa* (an Irish equivalent of *tabu*, an imperative obligation to do something), to attend a feast to which he has been invited at Conchubar's instigation. The sons of Usna are then killed treacherously and Deirdre commits suicide.

From the Fenian cycle Yeats took the story of Finn's son Oisin, who spent three hundred years in the other world with the fairy princess Niamh, returning to earth but so disgusted by the puny nature of the men he meets that he throws a sack of sand (carried by two men with difficulty) five yards, but then falls from his magic horse and his three hundred years of age suddenly strike him. He becomes old and learns of the coming of Christianity. In his handling of the material of these Irish legends Yeats tended in his early Celtic Twilight period to soften the originals in his pursuit of beauty. In his middle period he treated them somewhat differently, and the narrative poems *The Old Age of Queen Maeve* (1903) and *The Two Kings* (1914) show how he was stripping his verse of decoration and strengthening his handling of the material of the tales with greater realism. In his later period he looked back at his heroes rather mockingly in such poems as 'News for the Delphic Oracle' where the romantic fairy princess Niamh of *The Wanderings of Oisin* is described as 'Man-picker', or 'The Circus Animals' Desertion' where Oisin is 'led by the nose / Through three enchanted islands'. Cuchulain, however, is characterised as a model for the regenerated Irish in 'The Statues'.

Irish politics

Yeats kept politics out of his early poetry (indeed he greatly disliked a poem he had written on the occasion of Parnell's funeral in 1891, entitled 'Mourn – and then onward'). In his middle period, however, he began to write increasingly directly about his political feelings. 'Upon a House Shaken by the Land Agitation' shows how highly he regarded the aristocratic tradition of the Big House, while 'To a Wealthy Man . . . Pictures' is a savage satire on Irish patrons of the arts compared to the Italians of the Renaissance. 'To a Shade', addressed to Parnell's ghost, advises it not to return to Dublin where the mean of soul 'are at their old tricks yet'. 'September 1913' finds contemporary patriots lacking in comparison to those of the past who gave their lives in revolutions. 'An Appointment' resents an appointment made by a politician.

In 'Easter 1916' Yeats records the effect of the 1916 Rising on him: he realised the likely political effect of the executions of the Irish leaders. 'Nineteen Hundred and Nineteen' and 'Meditations in Time of Civil War' capture the hatreds and uncertainties caused by the contemporary situation in Ireland. 'Death' considers the effect of the murder of Kevin O'Higgins while 'Parnell's Funeral' finds Irish politicians of the 1930s wanting in comparison to Parnell. 'Come gather round me, Parnellites' was inspired by Yeats's reading Henry Harrison's *Parnell Vindicated* (1931), and is meant to emphasise O'Shea's attitude to his wife's affair with Parnell. (Yeats wrote in a letter of September 1936 to Dorothy Wellesley that: 'If Parnell had been able to raise £20,000 O'Shea would have let himself be divorced instead of [citing] Parnell' [as co-respondent]), which led to the divorce case, which in turn led to the split in the Irish party. 'The Curse of Cromwell' also goes back into Irish political history, but much further back, while at the same time offering a savage comment on a time when 'money's rant is on'.

In his Irish political poems Yeats sees history in terms of the men who make it: he had a sense of the romantic quality of the leaders of rebellions: Lord Edward Fitzgerald, Wolfe Tone, Robert Emmet, and John O'Leary are heroic figures in 1913. To them are added in 1916 Constance Markiewicz, Patrick Pearse, Thomas MacDonagh, James Connolly, even John MacBride. Then come the anonymous affable Irregular and the Irish Free State lieutenant and his men, in the civil war, and later O'Higgins, assassinated afterwards for his tough actions in it.

The Anglo-Irish of the eighteenth century follow in 'Blood and the Moon' and 'The Seven Sages': Dean Swift, Bishop Berkeley, Oliver Goldsmith and Edmund Burke, who shaped Irish thought in their different ways. Parnell, of course, is there in the *Last Poems* (which also includes poems on Roger Casement, provoked by Yeats's reading of Dr Maloney's *The Forged Casement Diaries* (1936)). There are the portraits of Irish leaders in 'The Municipal Gallery Revisited'. Pearse in 'The Statues', Mitchel in 'Under Ben Bulben' and The O'Rahilly in 'The O'Rahilly' remind us of how stocked Yeats's mind was with the human images of history. They are loaded images, symbols which reverberate in the minds of Irish readers just as, say, Nelson or Churchill reverberate in the English mind, Knox or Bonnie Prince Charlie in the Scottish, or Washington or Roosevelt in the American. And when you think of Yeats in a political capacity, remembering his membership of the secret Irish Republican Brotherhood in his youth and his hopes of uniting the Irish political parties when he was President of the 1798 Association, as well as his more conservative attitudes as a Senator of the Irish Free State, then read his poem 'Politics' and remember that he was, primarily and finally, a poet!

Love

Yeats's early love poetry is defeatist, mournful. Some of the titles indicate this: 'The Pity of Love', 'The Sorrow of Love', 'He Mourns for the Change that has come upon Him and his Beloved, and longs for the End of the World'. The poetry is sensitive, delicate, concerned with beauty. For examples of this see 'The Lover tells of the Rose in his Heart' or 'The White Birds' or 'He remembers forgotten Beauty' which are poems of longing, and of despair only to be solved in ways that are not the normal ones of this life. This melancholia pervades 'He Hears the Cry of the Sedge', this defeatism 'He wishes his Beloved were Dead', while 'He wishes for the Cloths of Heaven' is the quintessence of poetic devotion. Its keynote is the conjunction of poverty and dreaming; dreaming is all that is possible, along with devotion.

In the early poetry, most of it written to Maud Gonne, the symbol of the Rose is used – as it has been in love poetry over the ages – for her, though it has other meanings (to be discussed later). The poem 'Adam's Curse' (not included in *Selected Poems*), however, marked the passing of the years; a note of weariness intrudes:

I strove
To love you in the old high way of love;
That it had all seemed happy, and yet we'd grown
As weary-hearted as that hollow moon.

Despite the devotion of 'Red Hanrahan's Song about Ireland' (an earlier poem; see notes on it), other poems in *In the Seven Woods* share this change in the poet's attitude. 'The Folly of being Comforted' records the 'Well-beloved's hair has threads of grey, / And little shadows come about her eyes'. Poems such as 'The Arrow', 'Never Give All the Heart', 'O Do not love too long' have a sense of failure about them.

This was made clear in the poems written after Maud Gonne married John MacBride in 1903. Now there could be no hope: poems such as 'A Woman Homer Sung', and 'Peace' (not included in *Selected Poems*) and, especially, 'No Second Troy' use the Homeric symbolism of Helen of Troy for Maud Gonne (also used earlier in 'The Sorrow of Love'), and this continues later in the poem 'A Prayer for my Daughter' to stress the dangers inherent in women who are beautiful but do not make good marriages. These poems of the middle period may be disillusioned in that they record his past love for Maud Gonne, but they do this generously and impressively, as in 'Her Praise', 'The People' or 'Broken Dreams'.

The poems written to Maud Gonne's daughter Iseult, 'To a Child Dancing in the Winds', 'To a Young Beauty', 'To a Young Girl', and 'Michael Robartes and the Dancer', tend to offer advice, though 'Two Songs of a Fool' does realise Iseult is no longer his responsibility.

These are poems about love (or sometimes sexual relationships) which occasionally revert intensely to Maud Gonne ('Does the imagination dwell the most / Upon a woman won or woman lost?' in 'The Tower'); others in *A Man Young and Old* and the corresponding series *A Woman Young and Old*, as well as in *Words for Music Perhaps*, are less obviously related to the poet himself. The last poems, however, still celebrate Maud, in 'A Bronze Head', in 'Long-Legged Fly' and, especially, in 'Beautiful Lofty Things' in which his initial impression on first meeting her in 1889 recurs – she is goddess-like, 'Pallas Athene in that straight back and arrogant head'.

Friendship

Yeats tended to write on his friends after they had died: thus 'The Grey Rock' includes a tribute to Ernest Dowson and Lionel Johnson, the poets of the eighteen-nineties 'who never made a poorer song' that they 'might have a heavier purse'. O'Leary was praised in 'September 1913'. 'Friends', however, did praise three living women, Mrs 'Shakespear (with whom he had an affair in 1896; this was his first experience of love, brought to an end by Maud Gonne; he and Mrs Shakespear remained friends), Lady Gregory and Maud Gonne; but the identities of the first two must have seemed sufficiently disguised to allow him to publish the poem. The fine elegies 'In Memory of Major Robert Gregory' and 'An Irish Airman foresees his Death' mark a great development in a capacity to express appreciation with dignity, with a detachment that heightens the sense of loss, an awareness of the nature of the dead man, so different from Yeats's own. That 'enquiring man' John Synge is praised in poems, though Yeats wrote more largely of him in prose. 'The New Faces' begins Yeats's elevation of Lady Gregory, the achievement of whose life was given magnificent praise in the two poems 'Coole Park, 1929' and 'Coole Park and Ballylee, 1931'. He achieves a vignette of her bravery in 'Beautiful Lofty Things', and in 'The Municipal Gallery Revisited' he links her with Synge and himself, making, in the final stanza, with justification, a proud affirmation:

Think where man's glory most begins and ends,
And say my glory was I had such friends.

Occultism, magic, religion and philosophy

'To Ireland in the Coming Times' puts very well Yeats's early use of what he learned in his wide reading of Indian thought, Theosophy, Rosicrucianism, Cabbalism, magic and mysticism. He thought he should not be thought less of a patriotic writer

> *Because, to him who ponders well*
> *My rhymes more than their rhyming tell*

Some of the poems he was writing in the eighteen-nineties had esoteric meanings which would not have been clear to the vast majority of his contemporary readers. 'The Two Trees', for instance, would have required a knowledge of the tree of life (given in Yeats's *The Secret Rose*); while the poem 'The Secret Rose' combines Christian and pagan ideas, and the symbolism of the Rose (also used to indicate Ireland and Maud Gonne and intellectual beauty) would not have been fully clear unless it was understood as the Rosicrucian symbol of the four-petalled rose allied with the cross. Rosicrucianism is the subject of 'The Mountain Tomb' also.

Yeats at times reverted to earlier interests. For instance, his interest in Indian ideas expressed in early poems (not included in *Selected Poems*) stemming in part from the activities of the Hermetic Society in Dublin and the conversations of a Bengali seer, Mohini Chatterjee, was caught up again in 'Mohini Chatterjee', and the influence manifested itself later in the person of the Swami for whose books Yeats wrote Introductions, and to whose friendship such poems as 'Meru' can be attributed.

As far as orthodox Christianity was concerned Yeats was often indebted to the Bible, but tended to read on what might be called its periphery. Thus, for example, he reads of Christian monasticism in two books by J.O. Hannay, *The Spirit and Origin of Christian Monasticism* and *The Wisdom of the Desert* (1904) and in Flaubert's *La Tentation de Saint Antoine*. He was interested in the legends attaching to St Patrick's purgatory at Lough Derg as early as 1900 when he read Denis Florence MacCarthy's translation of the Spanish dramatist Calderon's *Saint Patrick's Purgatory*; this was an interest which he revived in the 1930s, reading several recent books on the subject; it culminated in his poem 'The Pilgrim'. He was reading Baron von Hügel's book *The Mystical Element of Religion* (1908) when he wrote 'Vacillation' and had read several books on St Theresa. He had, of course, met Irish saints in many places in his reading of Irish literature, and his poems on one invented character, the Christian monk Ribh, in the nineteen-thirties may have been stimulated by conversations with the Irish dramatist and poet F.R. Higgins.

Philosophy

Yeats probably came to philosophy via the Neo-Platonics; he read Thomas Taylor's translations of Plato and Plotinus and later Stephen MacKenna's (see notes on 'The Delphic Oracle on Plotinus' and 'News for the Delphic Oracle'); he read Plato, some Aristotle, and, after he became a Senator he grew very interested in the Irish philosopher George Berkeley. Some of the philosophers he read were Descartes, Locke, Hegel, Nietzsche, and, among the moderns, McTaggart, Whitehead and Bertrand Russell. He had read a good deal about astrology, he read many mystic writers. He had also studied Blake, Swedenborg and Boehme, the two latter probably influencing his concept of the gyres of historical change. His father once reminded him that he was a poet, not a philosopher, but that did not prevent Yeats considering philosophic problems and, at times, invoking the philosophers he had read, as in 'Among School Children' where Plato thought 'nature but a spume that plays / Upon a ghostly paradigm of things'. Yeats, however, remains a poet rather than a religious or philosophical man: 'Homer is my example and his unchristened heart'.

A Vision

Three poems which anticipate the poetry written under the stimulus of Mrs Yeats's automatic writing are 'Ego Dominus Tuus', 'The Phases of the Moon' and 'The Double Vision of Michael Robartes'. Here are the ideas of the mask, or anti-self, and the phases of the moon. Yeats had been working on these ideas and they appear in his prose work *Per Amica Silentia Lunae* (1918). But after his marriage the automatic writing of his wife seemed to give some superhuman sanction to the ideas, and Yeats produced out of them the strange philosophy of *A Vision*, in which he arranged his views of history and human personality. There are many reflections of his reading in varied subjects such as those briefly sketched in the previous section. *A Vision* acted as a kind of scaffolding which enabled him to write poems such as 'The Second Coming' in which he contemplates an annunciation, a revelation heralding the coming of an age which will reverse all the achievements of the Christian era, itself brought about by an annunciation and the revelation, the birth of the Christ child in Bethlehem – the fact that the rough beast is to be born there emphasises the desecration, the anarchy, the terror that is coming on the world. 'Two Songs from a Play' have the same oracular, gnomic strength because they are written within a system of thought and do not need the poet to explain so much as contemplate and illustrate. 'Leda and the Swan' considers the union of god and human with all its consequence. The sequence of historical events beats through 'The Gyres' while in 'Lapis Lazuli' the poet faces the coming ruin with bravery.

These poems come from Yeats's constant preoccupation with the nature of life, and, particularly, with what happens after death. 'At Algeciras – a Meditation upon Death' puts it well:

> Bid imagination run
> Much on the Great Questioner;
> What He can question, what if questioned I
> Can with a fitting confidence reply

The theme runs through 'Vacillation', its desire to believe balanced by an innate scepticism, is contained in *Supernatural Songs*, is brilliantly compressed in 'The Four Ages of Man', and continued, too, in 'What Then?', with its insistent questioning refrain, and in 'The Man and the Echo' with its confession of ultimate ignorance of the future. And, towards the end, it was time for Yeats to emulate his Pollexfen grandfather who supervised the making of his tomb in Sligo; he did it in 'Under Ben Bulben' by writing his own epitaph:

> No marble, no conventional phrase;
> On limestone quarried near the spot
> By his command these words are cut:
>> *Cast a cold eye*
>> *On life, on death*
>> *Horseman, pass by!*

Style

Yeats is both a nineteenth- and a twentieth-century poet. Born in the heyday of the Victorian era he naturally was influenced by nineteenth-century romanticism: echoes of Shelley, Keats, Tennyson, Arnold, even Browning are there is his early verse, as well as influences of minor poets such as the Irish poet William Allingham and the pre-Raphaelites, Rossetti and William Morris. He had decided to exclude the contemporary, to deal in essences of beauty, to avoid ugliness. The early poetry is accordingly very delicate, gentle, dreamy. You might look at the predominating adjectives Yeats uses in the first three books included in *Selected Poems*, and consider how often he uses 'dreams' or 'dreaming'. Do you find some vagueness in these poems? You should try to identify the elements in the poetry that led to his being regarded as the poet of the 'Celtic Twilight', a term which was applied to much Irish writing, and came from his book *The Celtic Twilight* (1903). And perhaps it would be useful to pick out examples which show in what way he was a romantic.

Yeats used rhyme fairly regularly in his early poetry, gradually allowing himself an occasional off rhyme or half-rhyme. In general he worked hard at rhyme, and used many rhyme schemes – the one which seems most successful being his eight-line stanzas, rhymed as *ottava rima* and variations of it. You might look at the variations of rhyme schemes employed in the following poems, all of which have eight-line stanzas: 'In Memory of Major Robert Gregory', 'Sailing to Byzantium', 'Meditations in Time of Civil War VII', 'Two Songs for a Play'. You might also like to compare other poems with eight-line stanzas with these.

Another aspect of Yeats's technique to examine is his use of refrains, which sometimes build up an effect in a cumulative way, sometimes act as an integral part of a stanza. Scansion will reveal Yeats using iambic verse freely and trochaic metres less freely, with a rarer use of anapaestic or dactylic metre.

One of the most interesting devices Yeats uses is the repetition of articles, relative pronouns and copulas. He uses this repetition in an obvious but very effective way. You might look at 'Byzantium' for examples of very skilful repetition not only of monosyllabic words but of images also. He also employs contrast frequently: the tension of opposites, of self and soul, for instance, as in 'A Dialogue of Self and Soul'. And he is a master of the interrogative manner, leaving questions reverberating in the reader's mind, suggesting ironies, paradoxes, personal attitudes of joy or despair, philosophical or political problems, even making profound statements out of questions which encapsulate what has gone before, as in 'Nineteen Hundred and Nineteen':

Man is in love and loves what vanishes.
What more is there to say?

Yeats enjoyed the sound of words, and used them to create a rich texture in his poetry; you might notice his use of Irish place-names and the names of figures in Irish legend; he creates a reaction in his reader by the repetition of proper names from poem to poem. He repeats his symbols—of places, the tower, the winding stair, the lake at Coole, and Urbino, or of characters, Cuchulain, Deirdre, Oisin, Niamh, Plotinus, Pythagoras, Homer and Helen of Troy. He sets a scene economically, atmospherically; he rounds off a poem by returning to its starting point having enriched the whole concept. He has a firm architectonic control of his material, which came, no doubt, from his habit of drafting poems in prose and then working and reworking his verse. Look, for instance, at how he creates self-contained stanzas, in a poem such as 'In Memory of Major Robert Gregory', which are yet vital parts of the whole argument of the poem.

Part 4

Hints for study

WHEN YOU ARE STUDYING Yeats's poems you will find it helpful to read them aloud (as he did when composing them, often saying a line over and over again till he was satisfied with the words he had chosen and their ordering). Read the whole poem through. Often the initial meaning will become clearer if you do this, and you will have gained a sense of the meaning of the whole poem without getting bogged down by details. Then it is worth-while marking the words or phrases that cause you problems. You may wonder, perhaps who Red Hanrahan was in 'Red Hanrahan's Song about Ireland', or who Duke Ercole was in 'A Man who offered a Second Subscription . . . Pictures', or who was being addressed in 'To a Shade', or what were the gyres in 'The Gyres'. Here the notes and glossaries are intended to help you, for Yeats does refer to many unusual people and places and ideas. Of necessity the notes and glossaries must be brief but you can follow them by using dictionaries and reference books (some of the latter are listed in Part 5 of these Notes). You will also find that biographical knowledge of Yeats adds to your appreciation of the poems, (you will find Augustine Martin's brilliantly compressed brief life, *Yeats*, Gill and Macmillan, Dublin, 1983, and the present writer's *Yeats: Man and poet*, 2nd edition, Routledge, London, 1962, useful in this respect). You will also discover that knowing some of the history of Ireland and its literature will make your study more effective. Some helpful books on this aspect of the background are listed in Part 5. You will not find that all critics who write on Yeats are helpful, and you will do better to read the poems and make up your own mind about their meanings and merits before seeing what critics have thought of them. It is probably sensible to put down your first impressions when you first read them; you may well change your mind about them on later readings and you may subsequently revise your own views in the light of criticism you read. What matters, essentially, is to understand the poems; after this you can begin to decide which you particularly like or dislike, and then you can work out the reasons why you have formed these views about them.

You should make notes about the poems; some, however, are straightforward and you will not need to put down more than will help you to remember them and your ideas about them. Your notes may also include groupings of poems (titles would be enough), such as 'Celtic Twilight' poems, poems related to *A Vision*, poems about love, about politics, about the artist and the patron, about the future, and so on. By thinking of the content you will be able to trace changes and developments in Yeats's expression of his ideas, or to recognise repetition of themes or images or symbols.

When you have to answer examination questions be sure you read the instructions and the questions very carefully. Allow yourself some minutes to decide how to use the time allotted (and leave about five minutes at the end, to reread what you have written in case you need to revise any of it and to remove any careless slips). You should allocate time carefully: if you have, say, four questions to answer in two hours then you will have less than half an hour for answering each question, allowing for two periods of five minutes at the beginning and end of the whole period of the examination for planning and final rereading. Of course, you may not wish to spend exactly equal time on all the questions, but you do need to work out approximately how much time you will spend on each one and keep as closely as possible to this. It is very wise to look out old examination papers, and to answer one or more of them, taking the same time to write your answers as would have been allowed in the examination. This will avoid your being alarmed at having to write for, say, two hours or three when you may previously have worked for only one hour or half an hour. And this habit of answering old examination papers means that the transition from learning, from taking in information to that of demonstrating your knowledge, of writing down your own views in response to questions, will be a more natural one.

It is wise to plan your answers before beginning to write them out. But it is a waste of valuable time to do more than put down headings for yourself. You may find it useful to plan to have an introduction and conclusion (a brief paragraph for each perhaps) and then to work out how many paragraphs you will need to deal with the substance of the question. Having this kind of rough plan (you ought to know how much you can deal with in the time you have given yourself to answer the question) will help to keep you concentrating on what the question asks of you—there is no point dragging in irrelevant material: the examiner will not be interested in it. Your paragraphs should form part of an argument, so that your views follow logically and build on one another as they reach the conclusion.

Try to write clearly and legibly. Examiners usually have a large number of scripts to read, and so it is a matter of good manners to see that your handwriting is not difficult to read.

Specimen examination questions

1. What seem to you typical features of Yeats's early Celtic Twilight poetry?
2. Do you think Yeats was a good love poet?
3. Discuss Yeats's attitude to his friends in his poems.
4. Write on Yeats's use of the image of the tower.
5. What do you think 'Sailing to Byzantium' is about?
6. Contrast 'September 1913' and 'Easter 1916'.
7. Write on Yeats's use of the ballad form.
8. Discuss how Yeats used the material of Irish legends in his poems.
9. Write on Yeats's treatment of his family in his poems.
10. Do you think Yeats could be described as a metaphysical poet? If so, in which poems?
11. What does 'The Circus Animals' Desertion' tell us about Yeats's view of his own poetry?
12. Write on Yeats's use of the imagery of the gyres.
13. Discuss Yeats's use of invented characters.
14. Compare 'The Valley of the Black Pig' with 'The Second Coming'.
15. Write on Yeats as a poet of defeated love.
16. Yeats has been described as a symbolist. Write about the symbols you have found in his poems.

A specimen answer

This answer is not to be taken as ideal; it is meant as a guide to show you one way of tackling a question: what you must do is put down your own reactions to a poem or poems in such a way that your knowledge and understanding and critical appreciation are clearly demonstrated.

Write on Yeats's treatment of his family in his poems.

Yeats' attitudes may be considered under three headings: in relation (1) to his ancestors, (2) to his wife, and (3) to his children.

1. In the 'Introductory Rhymes' to *Responsibilities* (1914) he considers how, nearly forty-nine, he has failed to continue the Yeats family line: he is unmarried and has no children. He addresses his 'old fathers' and sketches them in brief vignettes (the poem is only 22 lines long). His great-great-grandfather was a Dublin merchant, who is mentioned as having a special privilege; his grandfather, a country rector, was a scholar who was a friend of the rebel Robert Emmet and kind to the poor. He then lists more remote relatives, mentioning a Butler (the name the Yeats family set much store by, his great-great-grandfather having married a Mary Butler from this distinguished Anglo-Irish family) and an Armstrong, his paternal grandmother being the child of

Grace Armstrong (who came from a military family). He lists the old merchant captain, his maternal great-grandfather and then his maternal grandfather, who terrified him when he was a child at Sligo.

He is trying to make his ancestors interesting, unusual: they are of the middle or professional ranks of society; he links them with the establishment ('free of the ten and four'), the nationalist tradition (Emmet), the Irish poor, soldiers (linked with the Battle of the Boyne, a watershed in Irish history), bravery (the bravado of diving overboard after a hat) and the power of fierce silence.

He also writes about his ancestors in 'Under Saturn', remembering his grandfather (presumably) as 'an old cross Pollexfen', a Middleton (his maternal grandmother was a Middleton) and a red-haired Yeats, presumably his father's father, who died before his time. This poem reflects on his leaving Sligo, 'the valley his fathers called their home'. He returns to the theme of his ancestors again in a late poem 'Are you content?', calling on

> those that call me son,
> Grandson, or great-grandson,
> Or uncles, aunts, great-uncles or great-aunts

to judge what he has done. In the second stanza of the poem he refers to his great-grandfather, the rector of Drumcliff in County Sligo who set up the old Celtic cross in the churchyard there (where the poet himself is now buried), to his grandfather, the rector of Tullylish, alluding to his horsemanship, to 'Sandymount Corbets', relatives who owned Sandymount Castle in Dublin, to his maternal grandfather William Pollexfen, to his maternal great-grandfather William Middleton, 'the smuggler' (the sea captain who dived after his hat in Biscay Bay in 'Introductory Rhymes') and to 'Butlers far back/Half legendary men'. He is still seeing them in terms of family legend, wondering if he has measured up to them, whether the work he has written compensates for his not having had children who would continue the family line.

2. 'Under Saturn' compliments his wife for 'the wisdom that you brought, / The comfort that you made'. He describes their double dreams in 'Towards Break of Day'. 'To be carved on a stone at Thoor Ballylee' records that the poet has 'Restored this tower for my wife George'. He pays a warm compliment to his wife in 'A Prayer for my Daughter', where he praises her 'glad kindness' ('Owen Aherne and his Dancers' had sketched the unlikely, indeed unpromising beginning of the marriage when Yeats's thoughts were on Iseult Gonne, whom he earlier asked to marry him). 'Solomon and the Witch' is a humorous account of aspects of the marriage, which, not least in the automatic

writing which went to the making of *A Vision*, proved so fruitful for Yeats. His 'happier dreams' that came true are recorded in the late poem 'What then?' and include 'wife, daughter, son'.

3. He had, like most parents, pondered what future lay ahead of his children, Anne Butler Yeats born in Dublin in 1919 and Michael Butler Yeats born near Oxford in 1921. In 'Meditations in Time of Civil War' (the Irish civil war, 1922-3) he contemplated in the first section, 'Ancestral Houses', what can happen to families, where the strong founder of a rich dynasty has built a house—'The sweetness that all longed for night and day, / The gentleness none there had ever known'—but the strength of whose family may vanish in later generations. He had, he said in the second section of the poem, 'My House', founded his family in the tower:

> that after me
> My bodily heirs may find,
> To exalt a lonely mind,
> Befitting emblems of adversity.

He turned directly to his children in the fourth section, 'My Descendants', and wondered what might happen to his daughter and son. Whatever does happen, he said, the tower will 'remain their monument and mine'.

'A Prayer for my Daughter' (there is a corresponding poem 'A Prayer for my Son' not included in the *Selected Poems*) weighs up the dangers of a woman having too much beauty, bringing in Helen and Aphrodite as examples of such women being bad choosers of mates (he is thinking of Maud Gonne and, perhaps, of Iseult also); he hopes his daughter will be courteous (he is thinking of Mrs Yeats in this stanza) and will avoid the intellectual hatred that comes from having (like Maud Gonne) an opinionated mind. He hopes that she will marry into a life 'Where all's accustomed, ceremonious'. Another poem to Anne Yeats is 'Father and Child' which is a joke about a remark Anne Yeats made about a schoolfellow.

These poems about his ancestors and his immediate family show Yeats to be very conscious of lineage, of what is passed from generation to generation. His ancestors provide a yardstick to measure his achievement; his wife and children are the domesticity he had wanted. Late marriage had brought about the happiness of having his own home—the tower, the house in Merrion Square in Dublin, and finally the house and grounds in the foothills of the Dublin mountains—and caused him to view the future with even more concern than he had displayed in the poetry of his early and middle period.

Part 5

Suggestions for further reading

The text

W. B. YEATS: *Selected Poetry*, ed. A. Norman Jeffares, Macmillan, London, 1962; (Pocket Papermacs), Macmillan, London; Pan Books, London 1974 and subsequent printings. This is the text used in the preparation of these Notes; it is based on the *Collected Poems* (1933; 2nd edn, 1950).

W. B. YEATS: *Poems of W. B. Yeats. A New Selection*, ed. A. Norman Jeffares, Macmillan, London, 1984. This is a larger selection of poems with fuller notes designed for A level and university students. The text is taken from *The Poems. A New Edition* (1984).

W. B. YEATS: *Collected Poems*, Macmillan, London, 1933; 2nd edn, 1950 and subsequent printings. This is a useful collection if read in the 2nd edition, which includes poems written after 1933 and up to the poet's death in 1939.

W. B. YEATS: *The Poems. A New Edition*, ed. Richard Finneran, Macmillan, London, 1984. This edition has 125 more poems than the *Collected Poems*; these extra poems are mainly early poems, mostly included in the *Variorum Edition*, and poems from the plays.

Other works by Yeats

Selections

W. B. YEATS: *Selected Plays*, ed. A. Norman Jeffares, Pan Books, London, 1974.

W. B. YEATS: *Selected Criticism and Prose*, ed. A. Norman Jeffares, Pan Books, London, 1980. Both these selections contain Introductions and Notes.

Complete texts

W. B. YEATS: *Collected Plays*, Macmillan, London, 1934, and subsequent printings.

Autobiographies, Macmillan, London, 1956.

Mythologies, Macmillan, London, 1959.

Memoirs, ed. Denis Donoghue, Macmillan, London, 1972.
Essays and Introduction, Macmillan, London, 1962.
Explorations, Macmillan, London, 1962.
Letters of W. B. Yeats, ed. Allan Wade, Rupert Hart-Davis, London, 1954.

Biography

HONE, J. M.: *W. B. Yeats 1865-1939*, Macmillan, London, 1942.
JEFFARES, A. NORMAN: *W. B. Yeats: Man and Poet*, Routledge & Kegan Paul, London, 1949; 2nd edn, 1962.
MACLIAMMOIR, MICHAEL and EAVAN BOLAND: *W. B. Yeats and his world*, Thames and Hudson, London, 1971. Well illustrated.
MARTIN, AUGUSTINE: *W. B. Yeats* (Gill's Irish Lives), Gill and Macmillan, Dublin and London, 1983.
TUOHY, FRANK: *Yeats*, Macmillan, London, 1976.

Criticism

CULLINGFORD, ELIZABETH: *Yeats and Politics*, Macmillan, London, 1980.
DONOGHUE, DENIS: *Yeats* (Modern Masters Series), Collins, London, 1971.
ELLMANN, RICHARD: *The Identity of Yeats*, Faber and Faber, London, 1954.
HENN, T. R.: *The Lonely Tower*, Methuen, London, 1950; 2nd edn, 1962.
JEFFARES, A. NORMAN: *A New Commentary on the Poems of W. B. Yeats*, Macmillan, London, 1984. This is keyed to both the *Collected Poems*, 2nd edn, 1950, and *The Poems. A New Edition* (1984); it offers comments on and explanations of the extra 125 poems included in *The Poems: A New Edition* as well as revised and expanded comment on the contents of *Collected Poems*; it succeeds the same author's *A Commentary on the Collected Poems of W. B. Yeats*, Macmillan, London, 1968, and subsequent printings.
JEFFARES, A. NORMAN: *The Poetry of W. B. Yeats*, Edward Arnold, London, 1961.
RAJAN, B.: *W. B. Yeats. A Critical Introduction*, Hutchinson, London, 1965.
STOCK, A. G.: *W. B. Yeats. His Poetry and Thought*, Cambridge University Press, Cambridge, 1961.
URE, PETER: *Yeats*, Oliver and Boyd, Edinburgh and London, 1963.

Collections of criticism

DONOGHUE, DENIS and J. R. MULRYNE (EDS): *An Honoured Guest. New Essays on W. B. Yeats*, Edward Arnold, London, 1965.

HALL, JAMES and MARTIN STEINMANN (EDS): *The Permanence of Yeats*, Macmillan, New York, 1950; Collier Books, New York, 1961.

JEFFARES, A. NORMAN (ED.): *W. B. Yeats: the critical heritage*, Routledge & Kegan Paul, London, 1977.

JEFFARES, A. NORMAN and K. G. W. CROSS (EDS): *In Excited Reverie. A Centenary Tribute to W. B. Yeats 1865-1939*, Macmillan, London; St Martin's Press, New York, 1965.

MAXWELL, D. E. S. and S. B. BUSHRUI (EDS): *W. B. Yeats 1865-1965. Centenary Essays*, Ibadan University Press, Ibadan, 1965.

PRITCHARD, WILLIAM H. (ED.): *W. B. Yeats: A Critical Anthology*, Penguin Books, Harmondsworth, 1972.

UNTERECKER, JOHN (ED.): *Yeats: a collection of critical essays*, Prentice-Hall, Englewood Cliffs, New Jersey, 1963.

The author of these notes

A. N. JEFFARES was educated at Trinity College Dublin, of which he is an Honorary Fellow, and at Oriel College, Oxford. He taught classics at Trinity College Dublin; he was Lector in English at Groningen University, Holland, and Lecturer in English Literature at the University of Edinburgh, then Jury Professor of English Language and Literature at the University of Adelaide, South Australia, and subsequently Professor of English Literature at the University of Leeds. He is currently Professor of English at the University of Stirling, Scotland.

He has written on and edited the works of many Irish authors, edited four volumes of Restoration Drama, Selections of Cowper and Whitman, and written on various aspects of Commonwealth Literature. His *History of Anglo-Irish Literature* was published in 1982 and he is at present editing an anthology of Irish Poetry. He is Honorary Life President of the International Association for the Study of Anglo-Irish Literature.